ORIGINAL PUBLICATIONS

HELPING YOURSELF WITH SELECTED PRAYERS VOLUME 2

EDITED AND TRANSLATED BY
BABA RAUL CANIZARES

HELPING YOURSELF WITH SELECTED PRAYERS
VOLUME 2

By Baba Raul Canizares

© ORIGINAL PUBLICATIONS 2004

ISBN: 0-942272-80-3

FIRST EDITION
First Printing 2004

Interior illustrations by Raul Canizares

Original Publications
P.O. Box 236
Old Bethpage, New York 11804-0236

Printed in the United States of America

Part Two: Prayers To Traditional Catholic Saints

| Prayer# | TABLE OF CONTENTS | Page# |

Part Three: Prayers & Incantations to Mythic Personages, Folk "Saints," & Personalized Objects

Part Four: Spiritist And Spiritualist Prayers

Part Five: Prayers For Specific Outcomes

PREFACE

Ten years ago when I wrote Cuban Santería: Walking with the Night, I wanted to emphasize the predominantly African-specifically, Yoruba-character of the religion, a fact often under-emphasized by a largely Latino community of Santería practitioners in the United States. As I demonstrated in that book, Santería is an initiatic religion-a mystery religion-and the language employed in its initiatory ceremonies, such as in kariosha, the ceremony in which a new priest is created, is Lukumi, an archaic form of Yoruba, an African language. In Cuba and other Spanish-speaking countries however, those Santería priests who chose to dedicate their practice to healing-instead of, let's say, divining-relied heavily on a corpus of prayers stemming from a number of non-African traditions. These prayers came from diverse sources. Most originated in Roman Catholicism and can still be found in one form or another in Catholic gift shops on the reverse of little pocket pictures of saints, or in collections of popular prayers. Another source for these prayers is the French Spiritist movement begun in the 1800's by Allan Kardec, which has become a force in Latin America under the name Espiritismo. The third source, representing perhaps the most mystical, magical, and practical aspects of these prayers, is to be found among the indigenous populations where Santería has taken root.

Many of these hybrid incantations such as the "Prayer to Shango Macho" and the "Prayer to the Seven African Powers" were first used in the city of Santiago, in eastern Cuba. In this part of Cuba, ritos

1

cruzados or "crossed rites" ("crossed" meaning "mixed," as in mixing Lukumi with Spanish) are popular among practitioners of Santería. Other prayers were composed in honor of historical or legendary folk heroes, such as the "Prayer to Jose Gregorio Hernandez," a 20th century Venezuelan physician who enjoys enormous popularity since his death in 1919. There are also prayers to archetypal spirit guides. Such as the "Prayer to the Congo Spirit," "Prayer to the Indian Spirit," and the "Prayer to La Madama," an Aunt Jemima look-alike representing the house "mammy" slaves that often took care of a white household's children.

When English-speaking people began to adopt Santería en masse after the Cuban exodus to the United States in the 1960's, the Lukumi aspects of the religion became easily adaptable to the new milieu, but the Spanish prayers used outside initiatory rituals, the ones traditionally used in more popular healing-or sometimes cursing-acts were not generally translated into English, largely because of the effort it would take to collect, translate, and catalogue these prayers. With this volume, I hope to remedy this situation, gathering for the English-speaking practitioner the same efficacious prayers available to Spanish speakers for many years, but gathering them between the covers of a single tome in order to facilitate their use.

Because many of these prayers have long-standing associations with Santería, I have whenever possible included information relevant to Santeros, such as which Santería demigod (orisha) represents which saint mentioned in a particular prayer. At any rate, with this book the English-speaking practitioner will not only find an invaluable aid to his or her practice, but will also find conveniently bound under one cover over 150 prayers that had formerly been available as single sheets sold individually and then usually filed away in a filing cabinet or haphazardly kept in three-ring-binders. As in the original versions, in the English versions you will find that some of these prayers are inspiring, while others are simplistic and even coarse. Some are uplifting, while others are obtuse. The powers of these selected prayers, however, is immense, and if used with focused intention and an open heart, they can be tools to help the suppliants attain whatever it is that they want. The weight of centuries in some cases, and of millions of ardent believers in all cases, make these some of the most powerful magical formulas ever written. May the Deity guide you to use this powerful book to your best advantage. So be it.

INTRODUCTION

Pray-Period! Don't expect anything. Or better, expect nothing. Prayer cleanses us of expectations and allows Holy Will, Providence, and Life itself an entry. What could be more worth the effort . . . !
—Thomas Moore

God is shining diaphanously through the whole world for those who have eyes to see.
—Teilhard de Chardin

Praying is nothing more than the realization of God's presence. St. James says that every good gift comes from above and comes down to us from the Father of lights (James 1:17). Each experience in prayer begins with an act of faith that God has already done so much! God knows our needs and our wants. He also knows the practical materialism at the root of our way of life, a pragmatism that measures success by material values, "I must see immediately in my work and prayer something concrete or otherwise the work is useless." That which I undertake for the love of God and neighbor I soon treasure as something that feeds my own importance, thus, the more detached I become in my prayers, the more richly my prayers are answered!

Prayer consists of a conscious relationship with one who loves us. It is basically a look turned toward God. It is a human being standing outside of the habitual idea he has of himself, the person that he thinks he is. It is getting down below that false everyday ego and getting into his deepest source where he stands before God, consciously turning toward his Source, his Origin. Prayer is something applicable to every human being, and therefore should be as natural as a baby looking on his father or mother's face.

The prayers I've included in this volume have been in use in Spanish-speaking countries for centuries. Although some have been translated to English, these translations have been haphazard at best. There is an old Spanish saying that goes, "el traductor es un traidor" (The translator is a traitor). This alludes to the undeniable fact that it is impossible to fully translate anything. The best we can hope for is an approximation. The most usual mistake "wanna-be" translators make is to confuse transliteration with translation. Idiomatic expressions prove most stubborn in this area. Take the Spanish saying "aqui hay gato encerrado," which literally translates as "there's a cat shut up here." The literal translation gives us no clue to the meaning of the expression, thus the translator would not use a literal approach, but would seek an idiomatic expression in English that would carry a similar meaning, in this case it could be either "something smells fishy" or "something's rotten in Denmark." To the charge that a translator is a traitor I must answer that although few of us speak Russian, millions of us love Anton Chekov!

In translating these lovely prayers, I've made it a point to retain the beauty of language found in the originals, and to respect the readers as intelligent, intellectual beings.

Before today, many of these prayers were to be bought separately in specialized shops called botanicas inaccessible to many practitioners not living in the big cities. Without further ado, here are more than 170 of the most popular, practical prayers in use in Latin America and Spain.

PRAYERS TO
CATHOLIC SAINTS
WITH SANTERIA CORRESPONDENCES,
AND
PRAYERS SAID DIRECTLY TO
SANTERIA ORISHAS

Most of the prayers featured in this section are directed to Catholic saints that have been syncretized (identified) with Santeria deities (orisha). These prayers are often used by Santeros in conjunction with African concepts. They also stand on their own and can be said by any person with faith, regardless of religious belief. Some prayers in this section are directed to the orisha and are the result of African-European syncretism.

STORY OF
THE CHILD OF ATOCHA
El Santo Niño de Atocha
Equivalent Orisha: **Eleggua**
Feast Day: **Jan. 6th**

The devotion to El Santo Nino de Atocha originated in Madrid, Spain, during the reign of King Alphonse the Wise in the 13th century. During medieval times, the Moors held large areas and battles between the Christians and Moors were commonplace. The Moors invaded the town of Atocha. Following a certain battle, the victorious Moors held a great many Christians captive, and prevented the adult villagers from visiting as well as bringing the prisoners food or water. Fearing for the lives of the prisoners, their families stormed heaven with prayers for relief. One day, a child appeared, dressed as a pilgrim of that period, carrying a basket of food and a gourd of water. The Moors allowed the child to bring food and water each day. The prisoners were fed, but the basket and gourd remained full. The child was not known to the Christians nor to the Moors, so the people concluded that the child Jesus, disguised as a pilgrim, had come to their rescue.

In artwork, the Holy Child often wears a brimmed hat with a plume and a cloak or cape ornate with the St. James shell. (During the Crusades, scallop shells were the symbol of holy pilgrimages and one European variety is still referred to as "the pilgrim" or "St. James' shell." Poets have written about their beauty and artists have admired their symmetry and grace.) In his left hand, He carries a pilgrim's staff

8

to the gourd of water is fastened, a pair of shackles, and a few spears of wheat. In his right hand, He holds a basket which generally contains bread or flowers. He either wears sandals or is barefoot. The Child is said to roam the hills and valleys, particularly at night, bringing aid and comfort to the needy, and thereby wearing out his shoes. He is usually shown seated.

The original statue of the Holy Child of Atocha was originally from Spain and now resides in the little town of Fresnillo, Mexico. El Santo Nino de Atocha is the patron saint of those unjustly imprisoned. He also protects travelers and rescues people in danger.

PRAYER 1
THE CHILD OF ATOCHA

All-knowing Child of Atocha, protector of all men, protection of invalids, divine doctor of all illnesses. Most Powerful Child, I greet you, I praise you on this day and I offer you these three Our Fathers, and Hail Marys, with a Glory be to the Father in memory of the journey that you made incarnate in the most pure womb of your most beloved Mother from the holy city of Jerusalem to Bethlehem.

For the petitions that I make today, I ask you to grant my request, for which I submit these deeds and in unison with the choirs of cherubim and seraphim, adorned with the most perfect wisdom, oh precious Child of Atocha, I am happy to offer you my supplication, I know that I will not be disappointed by you and I will be blessed with a good death in order to accompany you to the glory of Bethlehem. Amen.

STORY OF
THE CHILD OF PRAGUE
Equivalent Orisha: **Eleggua**
Feast Day: **August 7th**

The history of the Infant Jesus of Prague started in the 17th century when a statue of the Infant Jesus was brought into Bohemia (now Czech Republic) and eventually was given to the Discalced Carmelites in Prague. Since then, the statue has remained in Prague and has drawn many devotees worldwide to go and honor the Holy Child. Many graces, blessings, favors and miraculous healings have been received by many who petitioned before the Infant Jesus.

PRAYER 2
THE CHILD OF PRAGUE

This prayer was taught by the Most Holy Virgin Mary to Father Cyril of the Mother of God.

Jesus, you decided to become a child, and I'm coming to you full of trust. I believe that your attentive love forestalls all my needs. Even for the intercession of your Holy Mother, you can meet my necessities, spiritual as well as material, if I pray according to your holy will. I love you with all my heart, all my strength.

I beg your pardon, if my weakness makes me sin. I repeat with the Gospel "Lord, if you want you can heal me." I leave you to decide how and when. I am ready to accept suffering, if this is your will, but help me not to become hardened to it, rather to bear fruit. Help me to be a faithful servant and for your sake, holy Child, to love my neighbor as myself. Almighty Child, unceasingly I pray you to support me in my necessities of the present moment.

Grant me the grace to remain in you, to be possessed and possess you entirely, with your parents, Mary and Joseph, in the eternal praise of your heavenly servants. Amen

PRAYER 3
ANOTHER PRAYER TO
THE HOLY INFANT OF PRAGUE

Jesus, you decided for me to become a child, and I'm coming to you full of trust. I believe that your attentive love forestalls all my needs.

Even for the intercession of your holy Mother, you can meet my necessities, spiritual as well as material, if I pray according to your holy will. I love you with all my heart, all of my strength, I beg you pardon if my weakness makes me sin. I repeat with the Gospel "Lord, if you want you can heal me." I leave you to decide how and when. I'm ready to accept suffering, if this is your will, but help me not to become hardened to it, but rather to bear fruit. Help me to be a faithful servant and for your sake, holy Child, to love my neighbor as myself.

11

Almighty Child, unceasingly I pray to you to support me in my necessities of the present moment (mention them here). Grant me the grace to remain in you, to be possessed and to possess you entirely, with your parents, Mary and Joseph, in the eternal praise of your heavenly servants. Amen.

STORY OF
THE LONELY SOUL
Anima Sola
Equivalent Orisha: Eshu Alabwana

As the story goes, a beautiful maiden of Judea named Celestina Abdenago (judging by her name, a Roman) was assigned the task of offering water to those suffering on crosses. She gave water to the thieves on either side of Jesus, but not to the Lord, who condemned her to an eternity in Purgatory, a worse fate than an eternity in Hell because Purgatory is a place where souls go for a determined period of time until ready to be admitted in Heaven. Celestina was condemned to be the only permanent resident of Purgatory, watching all others come and go while she remains in Hellish torment, the loneliest of souls. Why such a creature inspires devotion is perplexing, but millions light candles to her on Feb 1st and reverently display her horrific image, a beautiful maiden chained to a stone wall, surrounded by flames.

PRAYER 4
THE LONELY SOUL
(Cuban version)

Cheerless Soul, Lonely Soul, nobody calls for you; I call for you! No one has need of you; I have need of you! No one wants you because they presume you are not welcome in Heaven, since you now reside in a Hellish region. Ride the best of horses and stride into the Tartar Forest, from where you shall take three branches from a special tree. One you'll give to the Spirit of Domination, the other to the unruly Spirit, and with the third branch I beg you to strike (say name of man here) So that he may know no rest until he lets me subjugate him to my whim and pleasure. He won't be able to find rest; not sitting, not laying down, not eating. Nor with a white woman or a black one, not with a mulatto woman, nor with an Asian. He won't be able to hold a conversation with any woman until he comes back to me like a dog to its master, humbled at my feet. AMEN

This prayer is to be recited at noon and midnight and an oil lamp should be kept lit behind the door until the desired end is reached.

PRAYER 5
ANOTHER PRAYER TO
THE LONELY SOUL
(Mexico)

Oh Lord, I offer my prayers for the salvation of the Lonely Soul. With your Divine Majesty and Love Direct your Merciful Eyes to the Lonely Soul, Amen

STORY OF
SAINT ANTHONY
Equivalent Orisha: **Eleggua**
Feast Day: **June 13th**

Born at Lisbon, 1195; died at Vercelli, 13 June, 1231 his father was Martin Bouillon, descendant of the renowned Godfrey de Bouillon, commander of the First Crusade, and his mother, Theresa Tavejra, descendant of Froila I, fourth king of Asturia. At the age of fifteen, joined the Canons Regular of St. Augustine, in the convent of St. Vincent, just outside the city walls (1210). Two years later to avoid being distracted by relatives and friends, who frequently came to visit him, he betook himself with permission of his superior to the Convent of Santa Croce in Cóimbra (1212), where he remained for eight years, occupying his time mainly with study and prayer. Gifted with an excellent understanding and a prodigious memory, he soon gathered from the Sacred Scriptures and the writings of the Holy Fathers a treasure of theological knowledge.

In the year 1220, having seen conveyed into the Church of Santa Croce the bodies of the first Franciscan martyrs, who had suffered death at Morocco, 16 January of the same year, he too was inflamed with the desire of martyrdom, and resolved to become a Friar Minor, that he might preach the Faith to the Saracens and suffer for Christ's sake. Having confided his intention to some of the brethren of the convent of Olivares (near Cóimbra), who came to beg alms at the Abbey of the Canons Regular, he received from their hands the Franciscan habit in the same Convent of Santa Croce. Thus Ferdinand (his baptismal name) left the Canons Regular of St. Augustine to join the Order of Friars Minor, taking at the same time the new name of Anthony.

St. Anthony is known as a sublime preacher, a miracle-worker who understood the language of dumb beasts, the man who played with a materialized Child Jesus, and the second most popular Franciscab saint, after Francis himself. He is the patron saint of marriage, of animals, and of finding lost things.

PRAYER 6
ST. ANTHONY

Oh Wondrous Saint Anthony, glorious as demonstrated by thy miracles' renown and by the gesture of Our Lord, who came to you as a little child to be held in thine arms. Obtain for me from Our Lord's great bounty the grace I ardently wish for in the depths of my heart. Thou who was so loving towards the lowliest of the lows, look not upon my unworthiness, but to the Glory of God that may be again magnified by the granting of this wish_____ . Amen

PRAYER 7
ANOTHER PRAYER TO
ST. ANTHONY

Oh most glorious St. Anthony, miraculous saint! You who have helped so many, I need your help in this matter_____. In my hand I hold your image as I ask that you make sure justice is fair to me. Comfort me in this hour of need, grant my petition with trust, Amen. (Make the sign of the Cross).

STORY OF
OUR LADY OF CHARITY
Nuestra Señora de la Caridad del Cobre
Equivalent Orisha: **Oshún**   Feast Day: **September 8th**

The legend of the three "Juans" notwithstanding, the real discoverers of the wooden image we have come to know as La Caridad del Cobre were two young Indians named "Hoyos" and a ten-year-old slave who were gathering salt at the shore of the Bay of Nipe in 1628. They were caught by a storm, taking refuge on a nearby cave. After the storm, they saw an object floating on the water that they thought was a dead bird, getting closer, they saw that it was an image of Mary floating on a plank where the words "I am the Virgin of Charity" were written on it.

Pope Benedict XV declared her the patron saint of Cuba, John Paul II rededicated the island to her in 1998.

PRAYER 8
OUR LADY OF CHARITY
TOWNSHIP OF EL COBRE, CUBA

According to tradition, this prayer was revealed to the three fishermen named "Juan" (Juan Odio, Juan Indio, and Juan Esclavo) who were saved by the Virgin from a raging storm; they were told to give it to women in need of protection. Juan Odio was a Caucasian, Juan Indio a native American, and Juan Esclavo an African. Together they represented the reality of the races found amidst Cuba's population in the 1620's, when the prayer was first told.

Know ye, my beloved children, that I am the Queen Mother of Almighty God; all those who believe in my great power and become my devotees must always carry my likeness as a relic on their persons to keep them company in their moments of greatest needs. I will free them from any evil threats, from unexpected death, from the bites of rabid dogs, and from attacks of wild beasts; I will also keep them from suffering unexpected accidents. A lone woman carrying my likeness shan't be scared, for she won't be bothered by phantasms as long as she says: "La Caridad is with me! Amen, Jesus!." "Juan Esclavo!"-said Our Lady- "Give this prayer, written on a piece of paper, to a woman having a hard time giving birth, along with the Holy Cross and the Gospels, so that even under the most heinous pain, if she puts this prayer on top of her stomach, and does the sign of the cross over the prayer, in remembrance of the Seven Great Pains I suffered during the birth of Our Lord, pains that were blessed by God Himself, blessings which I'll pass on to the expectant mother who remembers me during her hour of need." Amen, Jesus.

STORY OF
SAINT BARBARA
Equivalent Orisha: **Shango**
Feast Day: **Dec. 4th**

St. Barbara was the extremely beautiful daughter of a wealthy heathen named Dioscorus, who lived near Nicomedia in Asia Minor. Because of her singular beauty and fearful that she be demanded in marriage and taken away from him, he jealously shut her up in a tower to protect her from the outside world.

Shortly before embarking on a journey, he commissioned a sumptuous bathhouse to be built for her, personally approving the two-window design before he departed. As her belief became firm, she directed that the builders redesign the bathhouse her father had planned, adding another window so that the three windows might symbolize the Holy Trinity.

When her father returned, he was enraged at the changes and infuriated when Barbara acknowledged that she was a Christian. He dragged her before the prefect of the province, named Marcian, who decreed that she be tortured and put to death by beheading. Dioscorus himself carried out the death sentence. On his way home he was struck by lightning and killed.

Saint Barbara died on December 4th, 306 A.D. She was venerated as early as the seventh century. The legend of the lightning bolt which struck down her persecutor caused her to be regarded as the patron saint in time of danger from thunderstorms, fires, and sudden death.

When gunpowder made its appearance in the Western world, Saint Barbara was invoked for aid against accidents resulting from explosions—since some of the earlier artillery pieces often blew up instead of firing their projectile, Saint Barbara became the patroness of the artillerymen.

18

PRAYER 9
SAINT BARBARA

Oh God, keep away from me all those maleficent and miserable beings who would stalk me. I seek you out, St. Barbara, so you may confound them. Keep them at bay, and as I call upon you, offering my heart and life to you, divine Christian maiden whose bosom is welcoming of all good beings, cleanse me with your martyr's blood so that those who attempt to do evil to me will end up in Hell, Amen.

(This prayer is to be read on Tuesdays and Fridays. After each reading, three Our Fathers and three Hail Marys are to be recited. The prayer should be done a total of six times over a three-week period for protection).

STORY OF
OUR LADY OF MERCY
La Virgen de las Mercedes
Equivalent Orisha: **Obatala**
Feast Day: **Sept. 24th**

In the year 1218, St. Peter Nolasco and James I, King of Aragon and Catalonia, experienced separately a vision of the Most Holy Virgin who asked them to found a religious order dedicated to rescuing the many Christian captives held by the Moslems. This Order of Our Lady of Mercy, approved as a military order in 1235 by Pope Gregory IX, was able to liberate thousands of Christian prisoners, and later became dedicated to teaching and social work. The Mercederian friars' habit imitates the garments worn by the Virgin when she appeared to the founder of the order. The image of the Virgin of Mercy is dressed all in white: over her long tunic she wears a scapular with the shield of the order imprinted breast high. A cloak covers her shoulders and her long hair is veiled by a fine lace mantilla. Some images have her standing, with the child in her arms, and others with her arms extended showing a royal scepter in her right hand and in the left open handcuffs, a symbol of liberation.

PRAYER 10
TO THE MOST HOLY VIRGIN, OUR LADY OF MERCY

Most Holy Virgin Mary of Mercy, mother of God and by this august quality deserving of the most profound respect from angels and humans alike; I, one of your children, have from a tender age considered you my patron and advocate in heaven. Since then, every single boon, every grace and every good thing that has happened to me has been through your intercession. You are powerful in front of your most precious Son. Help me remain faithful to you throughout the days of my mortal existence, oh Virgin, so that in the afterlife I may merit being with you, thanks to your infinite mercy and glory, Amen.

STORY OF
SAINT LAZARUS
San Lazaro
Equivalent Orisha: **Babalu Aiye**
Feast Day: **Dec 17th**

The Lazarus of popular piety is a mixture of two characters named in the Bible. One is Lazarus, the brother of Mary and Martha of Bethany, friend of Jesus, whom he resurrected. The other Lazarus features in a parable said by Jesus, and is described as a poor man who lived off the crumbs of the table of a rich man, but on the other side was enthroned in Heaven while the rich man agonized in Hell. Somehow both Lazaruses became fused as one in popular veneration.

PRAYER 12
ST. LAZARUS

Oh Blessed and Glorious St. Lazarus of Bethany Protector and supporter of Martha and Mary. I call on you, oh beloved and always vivid spirit of grace with the same faith that Jesus called you at the entrance of your tomb, from which you emerged after having been interred for four consecutive days without showing any signs of impurities or decay. Oh, Holy Spirit, I call upon you with the same faith that God had in you to consider and grant what I ask for in this prayer. Amen.

PRAYER 13
PETITIONARY PRAYER
SAINT LAZARUS

Patron saint of the poor, I call upon thy spirit to ask of thee a favor. I hold in my hands a crutch and a medal bearing thy name. I call on thee to do justice for me at all times. I believe in thee, Saint Lazarus, in the name of the Father, Son, and Holy Ghost, may thou judge the merit of my request, relying on thy infinite goodness through thy intercession with Jesus Christ. Amen

Say your request, make the sign of the Cross

STORY OF
RAPHAEL
San Rafael
Equivalent Orisha: **Inle**
Feast day: **October 24th**

The archangel Raphael is the custodian of humanity. It is said that an old man named Tobias, who had a son by the same name, was suffering from a disease that left him blind. Walking around, the younger Tobias met Raphael, who was in human form. While bathing in the River Tigris, young Tobias was attacked by a huge fish. Raphael told Tobias to grab the fish, and he did. Raphael then taught Tobias how to make medicine out of the fish's entrails. With this medicine, Tobias cured his father and many others.

PRAYER 14
SAINT RAPHAEL ARCHANGEL

Oh Lord, divine Raphael. I come to you with joy and happiness so you may fulfill this need I have before 21 days have gone by. I want you to guide and teach me just as you guided and taught the young Tobias (at this point an Our father is said on the first day, two on the second day, three on the third day and so on). Oh Most loyal and loving custodian of my soul! Destined were you by Divine Will to be my guide and tutor, my protector and defender, may you never leave my side. I will give thank each day for the love and fealty you give me and for the many benefits you bring to me. You watch over me when I'm asleep, you counsel me when I need it, you feed me when I'm hungry, you keep danger away from me, you teach me to look towards the future, you keep me away from the wrongful path and guide me to the fortuitous road. You help me face God, for were it not for you I would have been burning in Hell a long time ago were it not for your intercession and prayers, which calmed the wrath of God. I ask that you do not abandon me in my hour of need, help me be moderate when I'm wealthy, free me from dangerous situations, help me resist temptations and don't allow me to ever be defeated. Help me, oh Raphael, Divine Physician, be faithful to God, showing Him that I am worthy of his consideration, thanks to your intercession and that of Our Lord Jesus, Mary, Joseph, Joachim and Anna. Amen

Invoke the Virgin of Mercy by saying a Hail Mary, and say an Our Father to the souls in Purgatory. Make your petition now.

STORY OF
SAINT THERESE
OF THE CHILD JESUS
Santa Teresita de Jesus
Equivalent Orisha: Oyá
Feast day: October 1

Educated by the Benedictines when she was fifteen she applied for permission to enter the Carmelite Order, and being refused by the superior, went to Rome with her father, as eager to give her to God as she was to give herself, to seek the consent of the Holy Father, Leo XIII, then celebrating his jubilee. He preferred to leave the decision in the hands of the superior, who finally consented and on 9 April, 1888, at the unusual age of fifteen, Thérèse Martin entered the convent of Lisieux where two of her sisters had preceded her.

The account of the eleven years of her religious life marked by signal graces and constant growth in holiness, is given by Soeur Thérèse in her autobiography, written in obedience to her superior and published two years after her death. In 1901 it was translated into English, and in 1912 another translation, the first complete edition of the life of the Servant of God, containing the autobiography, "Letters and Spiritual Counsels", was published. Its success was immediate and it has passed into many editions, spreading far and wide the devotion to this "little" saint of simplicity, and abandonment in God's service, of the perfect accomplishment of small duties.

The fame of her sanctity and the many miracles performed through her intercession caused the introduction of her cause of canonization only 17 years after her death, 10 Jun, 1914.

PRAYER 15
TO SAINT THERESE
OF THE CHILD JESUS

My Lord and my God I have realized that whoever undertakes to do anything for the sake of earthly things or to earn the praise of others deceives himself. Today one thing pleases the world, tomorrow another. What is praised on one occasion is denounced on another. Blessed be You, my Lord and my God, for You are unchangeable for all eternity. Whoever serves You faithfully to the end will enjoy life without end in eternity. Amen.

STORY OF
ST. JOHN THE BAPTIST
Equivalent Orisha: **Ogun** *(some say St. Peter)*
Feast Day: **June 24th**

Cousin of Jesus, baptized the Lord in the river Jordan, thus considered by Christians the greatest prophet. He died when Salome, stepdaughter of King Herod, asked for his head on a silver platter after having danced so well for the king during a birthday party that he offered her "Anything you want, even half my kingdom." What the evil young woman asked for, instigated by her mother, the queen, was the head of John the Baptist "on a silver platter." In this fashion, John the Baptist became a martyr before Jesus himself suffered at Calvary!

PRAYER 16
SAINT JOHN THE BAPTIST

Most glorious St. John the Baptist, precursor of my Lord Jesus Christ, handsome star of the best sun, Heaven's trumpet, voice of the eternal Word, the greatest among saints, lieutenant of the King of Glory, more a son of glory than of nature, and for these and all other reasons, most powerful prince in Heaven. Help me reach that which I hope to get, if it be good for my soul. If not, then give me perfect resignation, with abundant grace, so that God's friendship may be mine, thus securing for me the eternal joys to be found in glory, Amen. Our Father, Hail Mary, Gloria, Salve.

STORY OF
ST. FRANCIS OF ASSISI
Equivalent orisha: **Orunla (Ifa)**
Feast Day: **October 4th.**
Founder of the Franciscan Order, born at
Assisi in Umbria in 1182;
died there on October 3rd, 1226.

Saint Francis, the son of a merchant of Assisi, was born in that city in 1182. Chosen by God to be a living manifestation to the world of Christ's poor and suffering life on earth, he was early inspired with a high esteem and burning love of poverty and humiliation. The thought of the Man of Sorrows, Who had not where to lay His head, filled him with holy envy of the poor, and constrained him to renounce the wealth and worldly station which he abhorred. The scorn and hard usage which he met with from his father and townsmen when he appeared among them in the garb of poverty were delightful to him. "Now," he exclaimed, "I can say truly, 'Our Father Who art in heaven.'" But divine love burned in him too mightily not to kindle like desires in other hearts. Many joined themselves to him, and were constituted by Pope Innocent III into a religious Order, which spread rapidly throughout Christendom. St. Francis, after visiting the East in the vain quest of martyrdom, spent his life like his Divine Master - now in preaching to the multitudes, now amid desert solitudes in fasting and contemplation. During one of these retreats he received on his hands, feet, and side, the print of the five bleeding wounds of Jesus. With the cry, "Welcome, sister Death," he passed to glory on October 4, 1226.

PRAYER 17
SAINT FRANCIS

My Lord Jesus, Light and Splendor of the Eternal Father, you who with so many lights illustrated the seraphic St. Francis, defending him against the hellish hordes that sought to destroy him. I implore, oh Lord, that you may enlighten my thoughts so that I'll be able to recognize the sins that against your divine majesty I've committed, and that by with contrite heart confessing them, I may dedicate my life and death to you, Amen.

PRAYER 18
ST. FRANCIS'S PEACE PRAYER

Lord, make me an instrument of your peace;
where there is hatred, let me sow love;
when there is injury, pardon;
where there is doubt, faith;
where there is despair, hope;
where there is darkness, light;
and where there is sadness, joy.
Grant that I may not so much seek
to be consoled as to console;
to be understood, as to understand,
to be loved as to love;
for it is in giving that we receive,
it is in pardoning that we are pardoned,
and it is in dying [to ourselves] that we are born to
eternal life

STORY OF
ST. CHRISTOPHER
Equivalent Orisha: **Aganju**
Feast day: **July 25th**

Christopher, a very tall man, made a living carrying people across a river on his shoulders. One day a tiny child asked that Christopher carry him across. Midway, the child became so heavy that Christopher had to turn back. Astonished, he asked the child about his weight. "I have the weight of the whole world on my shoulders, Christopher." Understanding that this was the Christ appearing in the guise of a child, Christopher became a Christian, eventually dying for his god.

PRAYER 19
ST. CHRISTOPHER

Grant the following to those who invoke you, glorious martyr Saint Christopher, allow them to be preserved from epidemics and earthquakes, from the rages of storms, fires, and floods. Protect us with your intercession during life from the calamities that Providence may hold for us. During death free us from convictions, assisting us during our last hour, that we may reach eternal good will. Amen.

STORY OF
OUR LADY OF CANDLEMAS
Equivalent Orisha: **Oyá**   Feast day: **February 2**

Candlemas is also called the "purification of the Blessed Virgin" and the "Feast of the Presentation of Christ in the Temple." It is observed 2 February in the Catholic Church. Forty days after the birth of Christ Mary redeemed her firstborn from the temple (Numbers 18:15), and was purified by the prayer of Simeon the just, in the presence of Anna the prophetess (Luke 2:22 sqq.). No doubt this event, the first solemn introduction of Christ into the house of God, was in the earliest times celebrated in the Church of Jerusalem. The solemn procession of candles represents the entry of Christ, who is the Light of the World, into the

31

Temple of Jerusalem. When Our Lady is in this guise, she is known as "Our Lady of Candlemas."

PRAYER 20
OUR LADY OF CANDLEMASS
ALSO KNOWN AS "HAIL, O QUEEN OF HEAVEN"

Welcome, O Queen of Heaven.
Welcome, O Lady of Angels.
Hail! Thou root, hail!
Thou gate from whom unto the world, a light has arisen:
rejoice, O glorious Virgin,
lovely beyond all others,
farewell, most beautiful maiden,
and pray for us to Christ.

V. Allow me to praise thee, O sacred Virgin
R. Against thy enemies give me strength.
Grant unto us, O merciful God, a defense against our weakness, that we who remember the holy Mother of God, by the help of her intercession, may rise from our iniquities, through the same Christ our Lord. Amen.

PRAYER 21
THE SEVEN AFRICAN POWERS

Oh Seven Powers that are saints among saints! Humbly I kneel before your miraculous image, asking for your help before God. Oh Heavenly Father who protects us all when we are happy or sad, I ask you in the name of Almighty Jesus Christ for this petition (say your request). Now, once again I have peace of mind and material prosperity. Keep away from my house all harm and evil which may cause me hardship. May they never return. My heart tells me this petition is just and will be granted, if granted, it will glorify your name forever Jesus Christ in the name of the Father, Son, and the Holy Ghost. Listen, Shango! I call upon you, Oshun! Help me, Yemaya! Look upon me with grace, Obatala! Come to me. Ogun! Be good to me, Orula! Intercede for me, Elegua! All Seven African Powers in the name of Olofi, grant my request.

PRAYER 22
THE MOST GLORIOUS ELEGGUA

To the Lord of All Paths, illustrious warrior, immortal prince, I offer this humble prayer. Keep away from my abode all matter of evil and guard my home and those who reside in it when I'm awake or asleep, present or not. I ask Olofi God to bless you, Eleggua, beloved Lord of All Roads. Ashé.

PRAYER 23
PRAYER TO CHANGO MACHO

Oh spirit of Chango Macho, mysterious warrior king who has power over our future. Watch over me. I humbly pray that you light my path and bless my existence with good fortune and love. Allow me to succeed in my job, business, and at the games of chance you guide me to, so that I can meet my needs and be joyful and at peace.

I kneel before your image, I admire your power, strength, and wisdom, and I ask for your benevolence in the name of God Almighty. Protect me from all evil intentions, influences, and thoughts. I shan't retreat because you've vanquished my enemies!

Chango, guide and protector, Grant me _____ In the name of the Father, the Son, and the Holy Ghost, Amen

34

PRAYER 24
YEMAYÁ
Goddess of the Sea

Oh Holy Sweet Virgin Mary, favored by the Almighty King, Lady of Angels, Mother of God, Merciful Queen, Boundless in Pity. As in the days of old when the beleaguered went to your temples in search of sanctuary, so do we now seek comfort in your abode as you show us your mercy in many ways.

Sailors in great storms invoke your name as the Lady of Regla, thereby freeing themselves of fear. Before embarking, they give you offerings in your church in Regla, thus assuring themselves of safe travel.

Those being hounded find solace in your image.

The sick become well through your intercession, even those with fevers, broken bones, and anemic.

Bring health and strength to those worthy to receive it. We hope, dear Lady, that through your intercession we receive what we ask for in prayer. Although we know that, because of our faults, we do not deserve what we ask for, we beg you nevertheless to answer our prayers. Amen.

PRAYERS TO
TRADITIONAL
CATHOLIC SAINTS

STORY OF
SAINT MARTIN

Feast Day: **November 3**
Patron saint of barbers, innkeepers,
Peru, poor people.

Born 9 December 1579 at Lima, Peru, illegitimate son of a Spanish nobleman and a young freed black slave, he grew up in poverty. Spent part of his youth with a surgeon-barber from whom he learned some medicine and care of the sick.

At age 11 he became a servant in the Dominican priory. Promoted to almoner, he begged more than $2,000 a week from the rich to support the poor and sick of Lima. Placed in charge of the Dominican's infirmary; known for his tender care of the sick and for his spectacular cures. His superiors dropped the stipulation that "no black person may be received to the holy habit or profession of our order" and Martin took vows as a Dominican brother.

Established an orphanage and children's hospital for the poor children of the slums. Set up a shelter for the stray cats and dogs and nursed them back to health. Lived in self-imposed austerity, never ate meat, fasted continuously, and spent much time in prayer and meditation. Great devotion to the Eucharist. Friend of Saint John de Massias.

He was venerated from the day of his death. Many miraculous cures, including raising the dead attributed to Brother Martin. First black American saint.

Died 1639 of fever. Beatified 1873. Canonized 16 May 1962 by Pope John XXIII

PRAYER 25
SAINT MARTIN OF PORRES

Oh most merciful God! You gave us a perfect model of humility, abnegation, and charity in Martin of Porres, without looking at his lowly birth you made him great and glorified in your heavenly kingdom, amidst choirs of angels! Look at us with compassion and make Martin's intercession a reality for us.

To you, most blessed Martin, who lived only for God and for your fellow beings, you who so solicitously looked after the needy, tended to us who admired your actions and virtues and praised the Lord who so much praised you. Make us feel the effects of your great charity, praying for us to the Lord who so highly rewarded your meritorious acts with eternal glory, Amen.

PRAYER 26
SAINT JOHN BOSCO

O glorious Saint John Bosco, who in order to lead young people to the feet of the divine Master and to mold them in the light of faith and Christian morality, didst heroically sacrifice thyself to the very end of thy life and didst set up a proper religious Institute destined to endure and to bring to the farthest boundaries of the earth thy glorious work. Obtain also for us from Our Lord a holy love for young people who are exposed to so many seductions in order that we may generously spend ourselves in supporting them against the snares of the devil, in keeping them safe from the dangers of the world, and in guiding them, pure and holy, in the path that leads to God. Amen.

PRAYER 27
SAINT JUDE

St. Jude, glorious Apostle, faithful servant and friend of Jesus, the name of the traitor has caused you to be forgotten by many. But, the true Church invokes you universally as the Patron of things despaired of.

Pray for me, who am so miserable. Pray for me, that finally I may receive the consolations and the succor of Heaven in all my necessities, tribulations and sufferings. Particularly,

(here make your request),

and that I may bless God with the Elect throughout Eternity. Amen.

PRAYER 28
SAINT MICHAEL THE ARCHANGEL

Michael the Archangel, defend us in battle. Be our protection against the wickedness and snares of the devil.

May God rebuke him, we humbly pray; and do thou, O Prince of the heavenly host.

By the power of God, thrust into hell Satan and all evil spirits who wander through the world for the ruin of souls. Amen.

PRAYER 29
SAINT DYONYSIUS' LOVE PRAYER

O God the Father, good beyond all that is good, fair beyond all that is fair, in whom is calmness, peace, and concord; do thou make up the dissensions which divide us from each other, and bring us back into a unity of love which divide us from each other, and bring us back into a unity of love which may bear some likeness to thy divine nature. And as thou art above all things, make us one by the unanimity of good mind; that through the embrace of charity and the bonds of affection, we may be spiritually one, as well in ourselves as in each other; through that peace of thine which maketh all things peaceful. And through the grace, mercy, and tenderness of thy Son, Jesus Christ, Amen.

PRAYER 30
SACRED HEART OF JESUS

O God, Who dost deign mercifully to bestow upon us infinite treasures of love in the Heart of Thy Son, which was wounded for our sins;
grant, we beseech Thee,
that we who pay Him the devout homage of our piety,
may in like manner show unto Thee our due of worthy satisfaction.

Through the same Christ our Lord.
Amen.

PRAYER 31
OUR LADY OF GUADALUPE

Our Lady of Guadalupe, mystical rose, intercede for the Church, protect the Holy Father, help all who invoke You in their necessities. Since You are the ever Virgin Mary and Mother of the True God, obtain for us from Your Most Holy Son the grace of a firm and sure hope amid bitterness of life, as well as an ardent love and the precious gift of final perseverance.

Dearest Lady, fruitful Mother of Holiness, teach me Your ways of gentleness and strength. Hear my prayer, offered with deep felt confidence to beg this favor.

O Mary, conceived without sin, I come to your throne of grace to share the fervent devotion of your faithful Mexican children who call to Thee under the glorious title "Guadalupe" - the Virgin who crushed the serpent.

Queen of Martyrs, whose Immaculate Heart was pierced by seven swords of grief, help me to walk valiantly amid the sharp thorns strewn across my path. Invoke the Holy Spirit of Wisdom to fortify my will to frequent the Sacraments so that, thus enlightened and strengthened, I may prefer God to all creatures and shun every occasion of sin.

Help me, as a living branch of the Vine that is Jesus Christ, to exemplify His divine charity always seeking the good of others. Queen of Apostles, aid me to win souls for the Sacred Heart of my Savior. Keep my apostolate fearless, dynamic, and articulate, to proclaim the loving solitude of Our Father in Heaven so that the wayward may heed His pleading and obtain pardon, through the merits of Your Merciful Son, Our Lord Jesus Christ. Amen.

STORY OF
ST. CHARLES BORROMEO
Feast day: November 4th

Charles was the son of Count Gilbert Borromeo and Margaret Medici, sister of Pope Pius IV. He was born at the family castle of Arona on Lake Maggiore, Italy on October 2. He received the clerical tonsure when he was twelve and was sent to the Benedictine abbey of SS. Gratian and Felinus at Arona for his education.

In 1559 his uncle was elected Pope Pius IV and the following year, named him his Secretary of State and created him a cardinal and administrator of the see of Milan. He served as Pius' legate on numerous diplomatic missions and in 1562, was instrumental in having Pius reconvene the Council of Trent, which had been suspended in 1552. Charles played a leading role in guiding and in fashioning the decrees of the third and last group of sessions. He refused the headship of the Borromeo family on the death of Count Frederick Borromeo, was ordained a priest in 1563, and was consecrated bishop of Milan the same year.

He died at Milan on the night of November 3-4, and was canonized in 1610. He was one of the towering figures of the Catholic Reformation, a patron of learning and the arts, and though he achieved a position of great power, he used it with humility, personal sanctity, and unselfishness to reform the Church of the evils and abuses so prevalent among the clergy and the nobles of the times.

PRAYER 32
ST. CHARLES BORROMEO

Almighty God, you have generously made known to human beings the mysteries of your life through Jesus Christ your Son in the Holy Spirit.

Enlighten my mind to know these mysteries which your Church treasures and teaches.
Move my heart to love them and my will to live in accord with them.

Give me the ability to teach this Faith to others without pride, without ostentation, and without personal gain.

Let me realize that I am simply your instrument for bringing others to the knowledge of the wonderful things you have done for all your creatures.

Help me to be faithful to this task that you have entrusted to me.
Amen.

PRAYER 33
ST. CHARLES BORROMEO

O Saintly reformer, animator of spiritual renewal of priests and religious, you organized true seminaries and wrote a standard catechism.
Inspire all religious teachers and authors of catechetical books.
Move them to love and transmit only that which can form true followers of the Teacher who was divine.
Amen.

PRAYER 34
HOLY CROSS OF CARAVACA

Advocate against lightning, storms, and tempests.

About this sovereign cross, oh Lord, so miraculous and prodigious, a thousand elegant voices are raised in praise of its power, for no pen can write of its incalculable potency.

From the heavens above, choirs of angels descend to praise this cross, for so many miraculous deeds it performs, that it is truly a wonder.

Men, women, and children should carry with them the Cross that came down from the heavens to serve them as comfort; may it keep us from the claws of the fierce Dragon.

The lame, the crippled, the dumb and the blind, all find comfort in the Cross; so beautiful that Christ chose it as his spouse.

From heaven it was sent by the eternal Father, so we may ponder its mysteries here on earth.

The seraphim sing its praises with diaphanous voices; the cross made by Christ to serve as our comfort.

You may call yourself "most fortunate Caravaca," for you serve as banner for all that is heavenly, you, Holy Cross, where Our Lord gave his life.

All travelers travel without fear by land or sea, so long as they carry this cross with them.

Great are the mysteries hidden by this Cross; let us say, Blessed be the Cross! In this way hell trembles along with its denizens.

From unexpected deaths, fires, thefts, and many other dangers this holy Cross that found rest in the Arms of Christ saves us.

PRAYER 35
THE THREE
THEOLOGICAL VIRTUES

Oh Omnipotent God! Father of all that exists, Bountiful, Magnanimous, make me never reject FAITH, so that I may love and cherish you.

Oh Christ, Son of God, redeemer of mankind and exemplary model of humility and docility, infiltrate my animus with enough energy to make HOPE the comforting balsam that will help me complete my life's destiny with dignity.

Oh Most Holy Mother of Christ! Queen of Heaven and epitome of purity and virtue, you who prodigiously offered CHARITY to all who needed it, deign to bring to my heart the reflection of your radiant intervention so that I, also, may share with the needy some of the material goods I possess.

And with all of these virtues, FAITH, HOPE, and CHARITY, reverently effectuated, I beg you to grant what I ask in this prayer, if such a petition is for my good. If not, I will continue to practice the three virtues until I breathe my last breath, Amen

PRAYER 36
SAINT INNES OF THE WOODS
(Santa Ines del Monte)

Oh Sovereign God, infinitely graceful in allowing human hearts to find solace in your bosom, with the soft magnet of your divine bounty you attracted the noble SAINT INNES OF THE WOODS of Assis, who for your love rejected all of the vain promises that the world offered her, who gave up riches and even her own parents to embrace with valor the cross of mortification so that helped by your Divine Majesty she could become the spouse of the Lord in the seraphic order of her enlightened sister and mother Saint Clare, whom she emulated with fervor, becoming an exemplary role model of all of her perfect virtues.

Allow us, Lord, through your intercession, to be able to answer your call being attracted only by your ineffable goodness. Let us turn away from all false flatteries and worldly conveniences so that by imitating her virtues we may also embrace in this life the cross of mortification and, in this manner, we may also link our souls with your Divine Majesty in the celestial paradise of glory, Amen.

STORY OF
GABRIEL

"Fortitudo Dei", The Strength of the Lord. One of the three archangels mentioned in the Bible. In the New Testament, he foretells to Zachary the birth of John the Baptist, the Precursor, and to Mary, that of the Savior. Thus he is thought of as the angel of the Incarnation and of Consolation, and so in Christian tradition Gabriel is ever the angel of mercy while Michael is rather the angel of judgment.

PRAYER 37
SAINT GABRIEL THE ARCHANGEL

Oh most glorious prince of Heaven's court, most excellent Saint Gabriel, God's prime minister, friend of Jesus, and most favored by his holy mother Mary. Defender of the Church, advocate of mankind, you who so favors your devotees, teach me to love and serve, oh glorious Gabriel, and may you obtain from Our Lord for me that which I want and request through this prayer, for the greater honor and glory of the Lord and benefit to my soul. Amen.

With great confidence and devotion, ask now for the favor you seek.

PRAYER 38
ANOTHER PRAYER TO
SAINT GABRIEL THE ARCHANGEL

O God,
who from among all your angels
chose the Archangel Gabriel
to announce the mystery of the Incarnation,
mercifully grant that we
who solemnly remember him on earth
may feel the benefit of his patronage in heaven,
who lives and reigns for ever and ever.
Amen.

PRAYER 39
BEFORE A CRUCIFIX

Behold, O kind and most sweet Jesus, I cast myself upon my knees in Your sight, and with the most fervent desire of my soul I pray and beseech You that You would impress upon my heart lively sentiments of Faith, Hope and Charity, true repentance for my sins and a firm purpose of amendment, while with deep affection and grief of soul I ponder within myself and mentally contemplate Your five most precious wounds, having before my eyes that which David spoke in prophecy of You, O good Jesus: they have pierced my hands and feet, they have numbered all my bones.

STORY OF
THE POWERFUL
HAND OF GOD

The upward-pointing late Roman Hand of Power talisman continues in popularity today in the form of the Roman Catholic Powerful Hand (Mano Poderosa in Spanish) which is sold on holy cards and applied to votive candles. The meaning of the hand is the same as in ancient times - magical protection and benediction - but in the modern Catholic version, the fingers are all stretched upright, as is the thumb, and various saints and angels are standing on and around the digits

PRAYER 40
THE POWERFUL HAND OF GOD

(Say your request, then read the prayer)

Here I come with the faith of a Christian soul looking for your mercy while under such anguished circumstances. Leave me not without your shelter. If a door opens to me that would not serve me, let it be your Powerful Hand that shuts it for me! And if such door leads to my happiness and the peace I have longed for, then by all means leave it open. At your feet I leave this plea, from a soul so hurt by fate that without your Powerful Hand it cannot think of fighting. Oh God, please forgive any fault I may possess and grant me strength that I may yet triumph for your honor and glory, Amen. Our Father who art in heaven....

PRAYER 41
THE MOST POWERFUL ARM

(start off by reciting the Apostles' Creed)

Oh Powerful Arm, Jesus Divine, now that a sad mood envelops my soul, tearing my insides with desperation and woe, I come to you because you epitomize superior virtue, and all hearts are understood by your compassion. As you have taken control of your inner fires, you understand the difficulties faced by us mere mortals each day of our lives. You can also decide to what degree I am guilty and to what degree victim. Oh Powerful Arm, you who in search of our redemption became flesh and went through what those created by your hand go through, you who by choice experienced all manner of chance encounters with pain and suffering, allowing your precious blood to be spilled so that your doctrines and teachings could also be propagated throughout creation, receive my supplication on this day, grant me the following _____,

Finish with three Creeds, three Our Fathers, and one Hail Mary three days in a row. If at first you don't succeed, try again after allowing at least nine days to have gone by.

STORY OF
SAINT LUCY

A virgin and martyr of Syracuse in Sicily, whose feast is celebrated by the Church on 13 Dec. Lucy was born of rich and noble parents about the year 283. Her father was of Roman origin, but his early death left her dependent upon her mother, whose name, Eutychia, seems to indicate that she came of Greek stock. Like so many of the early martyrs, Lucy had consecrated her virginity to God, and she hoped to devote all her worldly goods to the service of the poor. Her mother was not so single-minded, but an occasion offered itself when Lucy could carry out her generous resolutions. The fame of the virgin-martyr Agatha, who had been executed fifty-two years before in the Decian persecution, was attracting numerous visitors to her relics at Catania, not fifty miles from Syracuse, and many miracles had been wrought through her intercession. Eutychia was therefore persuaded to make a pilgrimage to Catania, in the hope of being cured of a hemorrhage, from which she had been suffering for several years. There she was in fact cured, and Lucy, availing herself of the opportunity, persuaded her mother to allow her to distribute a great part of her riches among the poor. The largess stirred the greed of the unworthy youth to whom Lucy had been unwillingly betrothed, and he denounced her to Paschasius, the Governor of Sicily. It was in the year 303, during the fierce persecution of Diocletian. She was first of all condemned to suffer the shame of prostitution; but in the strength of God she stood immovable, so that they could not drag her away to the place of shame. Bundles of wood were then heaped about her and set on fire, and again God saved her. Finally, she met her death by the sword. But before she died she foretold the punishment of Paschasius and the speedy termination of the persecution, adding that Diocletian would reign no more, and Maximian would meet his end. So, strengthened with the Bread of Life, she won her crown of virginity and martyrdom.

PRAYER 42
SAINT LUCY
SPECIAL ADVOCATE FOR THOSE
WHO SUFFER FROM EYE MALADIES

Most glorious virgin and martyr St. Lucy, whose acceptance into Heaven the Eternal Father foretold early on by taking her as a worthy daughter during her childhood; the Sovereign Son choosing her as a loving spouse, while the Holy Spirit found in her a worthy Vessel. I Suppliantly ask St. Lucy that from the most Blessed Trinity you bring me a devout fervor, and that, just as your most fortunate soul began at a young age to serve God inflamed by the burning fire of his love, without withdrawing from such worthy pursuits, the culmination of which was your earning of the double crowns of virgin and martyr; may I attain, with your powerful help, a true love towards God so that by loving and serving him in this life, I may enjoy the privilege of seeing His joy in the sweet bye and bye, Amen.

With your precious eyes,
watch over us, lovely virgin.
Since it was God, sweet young damsel,
who made you a fierce warrior.
Lucy, you who rejoiced in Heaven's great might,
have your Divine spouse, guard over our eyesight.
Ask for what you want and recite three Our Fathers
and Three Hail Marys.

PRAYER 43
SAINT CIPRIAN AND SAINT JUSTINE

Most glorious Saint Ciprian and your most loyal companion Saint Justine, who since childhood were blessed with the ecstasy of watching the statues of Jesus and Mary, contemplating their perfections; thus did you console your cries. Get for me from such beneficent Mother and Son the ability to seek nowhere else for solace but from the contemplation of their greatness, to whom I gave up all my vices and bad habits, giving myself wholly to be worthy of their bounties. Grant this, beneficent Ciprian, as well as the special request I have this day_____.
Amen

PRAYER 44
OUR LADY OF THE HOMELESS

Oh, Sovereign Queen, How my soul rejoices in the vast greatness of your power and elevated status, although I am an unworthy vassal who deserved the ignominy your precious son, my redeemer, suffered for my faults and sins. Receive me, my Lady, give me shelter, you who are my firm stake during the dangers and troubles life gives me.

Give me the grace to be able to give you my heart with devotion thus keeping your standards, like being attentive and prompt when it comes to recognizing the divine laws which rule over life everlasting.

_____, I swear to God and a Holy Cross that you will follow me like the living behind the Cross and the dead behind the Light.

I say three Our Fathers to the Rambunctious Spirit (Espiritu Intrnquilo) so God will grant my wish.

Let all my past faults be erased from my soul, and I may get that which I need in order to attain tranquility and felicity as I traverse the august paths of eternity, Amen.

The first paragraph of this prayer is to be recited three times in honor of the three hours Our Lady suffered at the feet of Our Precious Lord, her Divine Son, while he hung on the cross. Then the whole prayer is to be read once from beginning to end.

PRAYER 45
THE MOST HOLY CHRIST OF GOOD HEALTH

Oh Sweetest Jesus, on the Cross Crucified, only begotten son of the Eternal Father and the Immaculate Virgin Mary! As a poor soul I come to you, most Benevolent Lord, as a sickly creature I come to you, the True Physician, the only Giver of Health, which is the true meaning of your Most Holy Name, Jesus; Do not permit me to stray from you before receiving comfort and solace at your Feet; grant that which I ask out of the goodness of your heart, and that of your Mother's; pay no attention to my faults, for you'd be forced to abandon me then: Look instead at all your merits, and then look upon me with pity, making me an heir of your Divine Glory.

Because of your merits I'll be able to reach that which I would have never been able to reach. From this moment on I offer you my most heartfelt thanks for keeping me in your mercy, which will be forever praised, Amen.

PRAYER 46
THE NEEDY

Oh God Almighty, Supreme Maker of the Universe! Forgive this Mortal if I have somehow offended you because of my ignorance. You who everything sees and by your infinite wisdom know, look upon the needs I have on this day and help me obtain my daily bread by way of honorable work or any other way that does not weigh heavily on my conscience.

Heed my plea, Oh Lord! Which I make from my heart, with the desire not to be delinquent in the performing of my duties and let those who owe me also keep their promises, so that my sustenance and that of my family will be taken care of, or my ideas can come to fruition if they be for my betterment and that of humanity.

Give me the strength to continue to face these trials that weaken my body and my spirit, do this for me not because I'm proud, My God, but to make my mission tolerable as I deal with all the unexpected obstacles in *my way placed without having to derail from my path.*

I thank you, Lord, for your infinite bounty, for no one can doubt your mercy, and I know you will help me realize my idea, or the acquisition of the job I need, Amen.

PRAYER 47
THE GUARDIAN ANGEL

Protecting spirit who watches over me incessantly, you whose mission it is to guard me, whether because it brings you joy to do good, or because by so doing your spirit advances becomes pure, save me. During the night, as my spirit goes out into the unknown, take me where my dear departed are, so that they may help me by teaching me lessons I need to learn in order to deal with the problems of my life. Make suggestions to my imagination, giving it solutions to problems I will face during my waking hours.

Help me gain strength by observing nature, help me raise my tired spirit from the new battles it has met, battles that have weakened my hopes. Amen

STORY OF
ST. APARICIO
Patron Saint of Animals   Feast Day: July 27

Born in Galicia, Spain, in the 1500's, Sebastian de Aparicio was a farmer and a lover of animals who had tremendous powers of communication with wild beasts. He later went to Mexico, where he became a Franciscan monk. He died at the age of 95, his body remains intact.

PRAYER 48
ST. APARICIO

Although St. Aparicio, beatified by the Catholic Church in 1787, was a real person, his prayer seems to work with the principle of like produces like, thus, he is invoked to find lost articles because his name is "Aparicio, "similar to the Spanish word for "it was found, "APARECIO!

I pray to you, Saint Aparicio, that just as the Child God appeared through your power and patience, that which I lost and now look for may also appear as I call on your glorious name; may all my valuable lost articles reappear, as I travel through dangerous passages, may my guardian angel appear: Help me so as I thrice say the word "APPEAR!" My lost articles will appear, by way of Saint Aparicio's intercession. May all obstacles fall away by the power of Saint Aparicio. Do not turn a deaf ear to my heartfelt petitions, as I sing your praises. Amen, Jesus.

May all Christians praise the name, of the sweet man Aparicio, Who with the strength of his hand, will find my missing lost issue.

STORY OF
ST. BLAISE

Patron of wild animals and healer of throat ailments

Feast Day: **Feb. 3rd**

In traditional Catholic communities, the Blessing of the Throats took place on St. Blaise's feast day, February 3rd. This day. Two candles are blessed, held slightly open, and pressed against the throat as the blessing is said. Saint Blaise's protection of those with throat troubles comes from a story that a boy was brought to him who had a fish-bone stuck in his throat. The boy was about to die when Saint Blaise healed him.

Very few facts are known about Saint Blaise. He was a bishop of Sebastea in Armenia who was martyred under the reign of Licinius in the early fourth century.

He was born in to a rich and noble family who raised him as a Christian. After becoming a bishop, a new persecution of Christians began. He received a message from God to go into the hills to escape persecution. Men hunting in the mountains discovered a cave surrounded by wild animals who were sick. Among them Blaise walked unafraid, curing them of their illnesses. Recognizing Blaise as a bishop, they captured him to take him back for trial. On the way back, he talked a wolf into releasing a pig that belonged to a poor woman. When Blaise was sentenced to be starved to death, the woman, in gratitude, sneaked into the prison with food and candles. Finally Blaise was killed by the governor.

Blaise is the patron saint of wild animals because of his care for them and of those with throat maladies.

PRAYER 49
ST. BLAISE

Oh enlightened soul of the Lord! Oh saintly pontiff and martyr, strengthened by God! You found delight in caves, wild beasts obeyed you, monsters protected you, deserts gave fruits to you, and loneliness kept you company. With innumerable miracles, you converted many gentiles to the faith of Jesus Christ. You saved those who had a bone stuck to their throats, becoming adept at performing such a miracle whenever a person so afflicted remembered to call your name! Look favorably upon those who call upon you with faith and devotion, so you may intercede for them , so that He who chose you and made you strong and glorious in heaven and earth will deliver us from all evil and the temptations posed by sins, as well as from earthquakes and tremors, and, most important of all, may we be delivered from eternal damnation, Amen.

Keep this prayer with you at all times.

PRAYER 50
SAINT ANNE

Good St. Anne, you were especially favored by God to be the mother of the most holy Virgin Mary, the Mother of our Savior. By your power with your most pure daughter and with her divine Son, kindly obtain for us the grace and the favor we now seek. Please secure for us also forgiveness of our past sins, the strength to perform faithfully our daily duties and the help we need to persevere in the love of Jesus and Mary. Amen.

(This prayer is begun and is ended by invoking the Holy Trinity. Make your petition and make the sign of the cross)

PRAYER 51
THE SACRED HEART OF JESUS

O most holy heart of Jesus, fountain of every blessing, I adore you, I love you, and with lively sorrow for my sins I offer you this poor heart of mine. Make me humble, patient, pure and wholly obedient to your will. Grant, Good Jesus, that I may live in you and for you. Protect me in the midst of danger. Comfort me in my afflictions. Give me health of body, assistance in my temporal needs, your blessing on all that I do, and the grace of a holy death. Amen.

PRAYER TO JESUS CRUCIFIED: Here I am, good and gentle Jesus, kneeling before you. With great fervor I pray and ask you to instill in me genuine convictions of faith, hope and love, with true sorrow for my sins and a firm resolve to amend them. While I contemplate your five wounds with great love and compassion, I remember the words which the prophet David long ago put on your lips: "They have pierced my hands and my feet, I can count all my bones." (Psalm 22/17-18).

PRAYER 52
THE SHOULDER WOUND OF CHRIST

O Loving Jesus, meek Lamb of God, I miserable sinner salute and worship the most Sacred Wound of Thy Shoulder on which Thou didst bear Thy heavy Cross which so tore Thy flesh and laid bare Thy Bones as I inflict on The an anguish greater than any other wound of Thy Most Blessed Body. I adore Thee, O Jesus most sorrowful; I praise and glorify Thee, and give The thanks for this most sacred and painful Wound, beseeching Thee by that exceeding pain, and by the crushing burden of Thy heavy Cross to be merciful to me, a sinner, to forgive me all my mortal and venial sins, and to lead me on towards Heaven along the Way of Thy Cross. Amen.

PRAYER 53
INVOCATION IN HONOR OF THE HOLY WOUNDS OF OUR LORD JESUS CHRIST

Eternal Father, I offer Thee the Wounds of Our Lord Jesus Christ to heal the wounds of our souls. My Jesus, pardon and mercy through the merits of Thy Sacred Wounds. Amen.

PRAYER 54
ACT OF REPARATION TO THE SACRED HEART OF JESUS

O sweet Jesus, Whose overflowing charity for me is requited by so much forgetfulness, negligence and contempt, behold us prostrate before Your alter (in Your presence) eager to repair by a special act of homage the cruel indifference and injuries, to which Your loving Heart is everywhere subject.

Mindful alas! That we ourselves have had a share in such great indignities, which we now deplore from the depths of our hearts, we humbly ask Your pardon and declare our readiness to atone by voluntary expiation not only for our own personal offenses, but also for the sins of those, who, straying for from the path of salvation, refuse in their obstinate infidelity to follow You, their Shepherd and Leader, or, renouncing the vows of their baptism, have cast off the sweet yoke of Your Law. We are now resolved to expiate each and every deplorable outrage committed against You; we are determined to make amends for the manifold offenses against Christian modesty in unbecoming dress and behavior, for all the foul seductions laid to ensnare the feet of the innocent, for the frequent violations of Sundays and holidays, and the shocking blasphemies uttered against You and Your Saints. We wish also to make amends for the insults to which Your Vicar on earth and Your priest are subjected, for the profanation, by conscious neglect or terrible acts of sacrilege, of the very Sacrament of Your Divine Love; and lastly for the public crimes of nations who resist the rights and teaching authority of the Church which You have founded. Would, O divine Jesus, we were able to wash away such abominations with our blood. We now offer, in reparation for these violations of Your divine honor, the satisfaction You once made to Your eternal Father on the cross and which You continue to renews daily on our altars; we offer it in union with the acts of atonement of Your Virgin Mother and all the Saints and of the pious faithful on earth; and we sincerely promise to make recompense, as far as we can with the help of Your grace, for all neglect of Your great love and for the sins we and others have committed in the past. Henceforth we will live a life of unwavering faith, of purity of conduct, of perfect observance of the precepts of the gospel and especially that of charity. We promise to the best of our power to prevent other from offending You and to bring as many as possible to follow You.

O loving Jesus, through the intercession of the Blessed Virgin Mary, our model in reparation, deign to receive the voluntary offering we make of this act of expiation; and by the crowing gift of perseverance keep us faithful unto death in our duty and the allegiance we owe to You, so that we may one day come to that happy home, where You with the Father and the Holy Spirit lives and reigns, God, world without end. Amen.

PRAYER 55
CONSECRATION OF THE HUMAN RACE TO THE SACRED HEART OF JESUS

O most Sweet Jesus, Redeemer of the Human race; behold us prostrate most humbly before Your altar (in your presence). To You we belong; Yours we wish to be; and that we may be united to You more closely, we dedicate ourselves each one of us today to Your most Sacred Heart.

Many have never known You; many, despising Your commands, have rejected You. Have mercy on them all, most merciful Jesus, and draw them to Your sacred Heart. Be You King, O Lord, not only over the faithful who never have gone away from You, but also over the prodigal children who have forsaken You; and make them return quickly to their Father's house, lest they perish of misery and hunger. Be You King of those who have been misled by error, or separated by schism; and call them back to the haven of truth and the unity of faith, so that there may soon be one fold and one Shepherd. Grant to Your Church, O Lord, assurance of freedom and immunity from harm; give peace and order to all nations, and grant that, over the whole earth, from pole to pole, may resound the words:

Praise to the Divine Heart, through which was brought to us salvation; glory and honor be to It for ever. Amen...

O Heart of love. I put all my trust in You; for I fear all things from my own weakness, but I hope for all things from Your goodness.

Most sweet Heart of Jesus, grant that peace, the fruit of justice and charity, may reign throughout the world.

The Promises of Our Lord to Saint Margaret Mary in Favor of Those Who Are Devoted to His Sacred Heart:

1. I will give them all the graces necessary in their state of life.
2. I will establish peace in their houses.
3. I will comfort them in all their afflictions.
4. I will be their secure refuge during life and, above all, in death.
5. I will bestow a large blessing upon all their undertakings.
6. Sinners shall find in my Heart the source and the infinite ocean of mercy.
7. Tepid souls shall grow fervent.
8. Fervent souls shall quickly mount to high perfection.
9. I will bless every place where a picture of My Sacred Heart shall be set up and honored.
10. I will give to Priest the gift of touching the most hardened hearts.
11. Those who shall promote this devotion shall have their names written in My Heart, never to be blotted out.
12. I promise You in the excessive mercy of My Heart that My all-powerful love will grant to all those who communicate on the First Friday of nine consecutive months the grace of final penitence; they shall not die in my displeasure nor without receiving the Sacraments; My Divine Heart shall be their safe refuge in this last moment.

(This prayer is optional and may be said after all Glory Be to the Fathers while reciting the Rosary.....)

O my Jesus, have mercy on us. Forgive us our sins. Save us from the fires of hell. Take all souls into heaven, especially, those most in need of thy mercy. Amen.

PRAYER 56
OUR LADY, ASSUMED INTO HEAVEN

Immaculate Virgin, Mother of Jesus and our Mother, we believe in your triumphant assumption into heaven where the angels and saints acclaim you as Queen. We join them in praising you and bless the Lord who raised you above all creatures. With them we offer you our devotion and love. We are confident that you watch over our daily efforts and needs, and we take comfort from our faith in the coming resurrection. We look to you, our life, our sweetness, and our hope. After this earthly life, show us Jesus, the blest fruit of your womb, O kind, O loving, O Sweet Virgin Mary. Amen.

PRAYER 57
OUR LADY OF FATIMA

Most Holy Trinity - Father, Son, and Holy Spirit - I adore thee profoundly. I offer Thee the most precious Body, Blood, Soul and Divinity of Jesus Christ, present in all the tabernacles of the world, in reparation for the outrages, sacrileges and indifferences whereby He is offended. And through the infinite merits of His Most Sacred Heart and the Immaculate Heart of Mary, I beg of Thee the conversion of poor sinners.

Fatima Prayer: *My God, I believe, I adore, I hope, and I love You. I beg pardon of You for those who do not believe, do not adore, do not hope, and do not love You.*

Mary, Queen of the Holy Rosary, pray for us. Mary, Queen of Peace, pray for us. Mary, Our Loving Mother, pray for us.

PRAYER 58
MEMORARE

Remember, O most gracious Virgin Mary that never was it known that anyone who fled to Your protection, implored Your help, or sought Your intercession was left unaided. Inspired with this confidence, we fly to you, O Virgin of virgins, our Mother. To You we come; before You we stand, sinful and sorrowful. O Mother of the Word Incarnate, despise not our petitions, but in Your mercy, hear and answer us. Amen.

PRAYER 59
THE SEVEN SORROWS OF THE BLESSED VIRGIN MARY

I. The prophecy of Simeon

II. The Flight to Egypt

III. Loss of Child Jesus for 3 days, later found in His Father's House

IV. Witnessing Jesus carry his Cross

V. The Crucifixion of Jesus

VI. Taking Jesus Down from the Cross

VII. The Burial of Jesus

PRAYER 60
OUR LADY OF MOUNT CARMEL

Jesus Christ, Savior of the World, Son of Saint Mary virgin, Most Pure and Blessed Lady who without pains gave birth to the Lord, pray for me to your Son so he may liberate me from all adversities and dangers of life, for you are the most beautiful of all, more than all flowers and all angels. Help me, crown me, fountain of mercy, temple of God, House of the Holy Spirit. Reach out and give me the grace of your generous son Jesus, so he may forgive my sins and bring to my soul true penance.

Intercede for me, oh Virgin Mother of God, so that all patriarchs, prophets, cherubim, seraphim, and all celestial beings along with the angels will pour their gifts by Jesus given over my soul. I hereby commend my soul to the Lord so that from now on all of its intentions are geared towards attaining the glory of God, Amen.

Jesus, Mary, and Joseph, Joachim and Anna, to you I commend my soul.

PRAYER 61
SAINT ISIDORE THE TILLER

Almighty and Everlasting God, creator and redeemer of my soul; I thank you for having provided us with your humble and blessed servant, Isidore, protector and advocate as well as remedy for all of my ailments, the result of the toils and miseries of this life. I hurt and am truly sorry for all the wrongs I've done against your divine bounty, and I hope that by the intercession of this saint you give me the grace to purify my soul of all faults so that, by saying this prayer with love, I may be worthy to obtain the graces that I'm seeking, so long as your Holy Name is glorified and my soul bettered. Amen.

PRAYER 62
OUR LADY OF FATIMA

Blessed be thy name. Protect me from vanity and deceit, for I know it is only in humility that I can hope for security. I know that in building my spiritual house, your blessing will be upon me today and always. Let me be an instrument in bringing joy to others, for that is surely the way my soul will be joyous.

PRAYER 63
THE BLESSED SOULS OF PURGATORY

Divine glorifier of souls. At the end of your passion, hanging on the Cross of torments, ready to die and in agony, you forced the last and seventh word : "In thy hands I commend my spirit." You then died and later manifested yourself in the bosom of Abraham in order to glorify with your divine presence the blessed souls for the pain of the pains that penetrated the heart of your sovereign Mother when she saw the light in your eyes dimat the hour of your demise. I commend to you, oh Lord, the Blessed Souls, so that when the pains, torments, and penuries of Purgatory are over, your divine hands will receive them in order to glorify them in heaven. And those who so often have tried to take your life with their faults, make it, most merciful Lord, that they truly repent at the hour of their deaths so they may say "In your hands I commend my spirit." And may I, my Lord, obtain what I ask for in this prayer if it be for your greater honor and the glorifying of my soul, Amen.

STORY OF
ST. GEORGE

Patron saint of England
Feast Day: **April 23rd**

He was born in Cappadocia of noble, Christian parents and on the death of his father, accompanied his mother to Palestine, her country of origin, where she had land and George was to run the estate. He was martyred at Lydda in Palestine (Nicomedia).

He held an important post in the Roman army - the rank of tribune, or perhaps colonel in modern terms - during the reign of the Emperor Diocletian (245-313). Diocletian was a great persecutor of Christians (from about 302) and when the persecutions began George put aside his office and complained personally to the Emperor of the harshness of his decrees and the dreadful purges of Christians. For his trouble, though, he was thrown into prison and tortured. He would not recant his faith however and the following day he was dragged through the streets and beheaded. It is uncertain whether he also tore down the Emperor's decrees as they were posted in Nicomedia. So he was one of the first to perish. The Emperor's wife, Alexandria was so impressed at the Saint's courage that she became a Christian and so too was put to death for her trouble. A pagan town in Libya was being ureides by a dragon. The locals kept throwing sheep to it to placate it, and when it still remained unsatisfied, they started sacrificing some of the citizenry. Finally the local princess was to be thrown also to the beast, but Good Saint George came along, slaughtered the dragon and rescued the fair princess. At this the towns-folk converted to Christianity.

PRAYER 64
SAINT GEORGE

Powerful knight, example to the humble, you defended us from vices with your lance, and also from the Devil, in order to transport us to glory. By the humility of God's glorious martyr, St. George, we humbly ask for the efficacious intercession of the saint to defeat all the dangers that sadden my existence, helping me anchor at a joyous port when fatigued, and to safely navigate the crossing over to glory, where I may eternally song your praises, Amen.

PRAYER 65
ST. CARALAMPIO
PROTECTS AGAINST AIRBORNE BACTERIA, SUCH AS ANTHRAX

God, Almighty Lord, in whose hands rest everyone's life and well-being, through the merits and intercession of your faithful servant St. Caralampio, priest and martyr whom you awarded with the crown of martyrdom which he won through his heroic faith and constancy exhibited while defending your Holy Name. Wherever a relic of St. Caralampio is kept, or his name is commemorated, there shan't be hunger, nor pestilence, nor contagion: We humbly ask you, Lord, as we venerate the memory of St. Caralampio, his martyrdom, and his admirable virtues here on earth, that we may be worthy of staying healthy and free from infection thanks to the merits of Our Lord Jesus Christ , with whom we'll rejoice in the heavens, where He reigns with God and with the Holy Spirit, Amen.

—Pray for us, St. Caralampio
—So we may be worthy to receive the promises that Our Lord Jesus Christ made.

STORY OF
ST. GERARD MAJELLA
Feast Day: October 16th

Born in Muro, about fifty miles south of Naples, in April, 1726; died 16 October, 1755; beatified by Leo XIII, 29 January, 1893, and canonized by Pious 11 December, 1904. His only ambition was to be like Jesus Christ in his sufferings and humiliations. His father, Dominic Majella, died while Gerard was a child. His pious mother, owing to poverty, was obliged to apprentice him to a tailor. His master loved him, but the foreman treated him cruelly. His reverence for the priesthood and his love of suffering led him to take service in the house of a prelate, who was very hard to please. On the latter's death Gerard returned to his trade, working first as a journeyman and then on his own account. His earnings he divided between his mother and the poor, and in offerings for the souls in purgatory. After futile attempts first to become a Franciscan and then a hermit, he entered the Congregation of the Most Holy Redeemer in 1749. Two years later he made his profession, and to the usual vows

76

he added one by which he bound himself to do always that which seemed to him more perfect. He was favored with infused knowledge of the highest order, ecstasies, prophecy, discernment of spirits, and penetration of hearts, bi-location, and with what seemed an unlimited power over nature, sickness, and the devils. When he accompanied the Fathers on missions, or was sent out on business, he converted more souls than many missionaries. He predicted the day and hour of his death. A wonderworker during his life, he has continued to be the same after his death.

PRAYER 66
ST. GERARD MAJELLA

Oh glorious Saint. You who suffered so much adversity and endured much pain, you who were persecuted and slandered, maintaining a remarkable calmness throughout your trials and tribulations, I ask you to give me some of your fortitude as I meet all challenges that life throws my way.

How can I attain the virtue of patience, oh holy saint, when the smallest work frightens me? When the most insignificant obstacles hurt and anger me? I must come to the realization that only through the path of abnegation is heaven reached. Guide me through life's difficult journey, St. Gerard, give me the strength to accept the crosses God assigns me so that afterwards I may deserve to be with Him in heaven, Amen.

PRAYER 67
SAINT GERARD MAJELLA (2)

O good Saint Gerard, powerful intercessor before
God and Wonderworker of our day,
I call upon thee and seek thy aid.
Thou who on earth didst always fulfill God's design
help me to do the Holy Will of God.
Beseech the Master of Life,
from Whom all paternity proceedeth
to render me fruitful in offspring,
that I may raise up children to God in this life
and heirs to the Kingdom of His glory in the world
to come.
Amen.

STORY OF
SAINT CYRUS
Feast Day: **Jan 31st**

Celebrated martyr of the Coptic Church, he healed the sick without charging them. His feast day is celebrated by the Copts on the sixth day of Emsir, corresponding to 31 January, the day also observed by the Greeks; on the same day he is commemorated in the Roman Martyrology. The Greeks celebrate also the finding and translation of the saint's relics on 28 June. Cyrus was a native of Alexandria, where he practiced the art of medicine. At the same time he labored with all the ardor of an apostle of the Faith, and won many from pagan superstitions. This took place under the Emperor Diocletian. Denounced to the prefect of the city he fled to Arabia of Egypt where he took refuge in a town near the sea called Tzoten. There, having shaved his head and assumed the monastic habit, he abandoned medicine and began a life of asceticism. During the persecution of Diocletian three holy virgins, Theoctista (Theopista), fifteen years old, Theodota (Theodora), thirteen years old, and Theodossia (Theodoxia), eleven years old, together with their mother Athanasia, were arrested at Canopus and brought to Alexandria. Cyrus, fearing that these girls, on account of their tender age, might, in the midst of torments, deny the Faith, resolved to go into the city to comfort them and encourage them in undergoing martyrdom. This fact becoming known he was arrested also and after dire torments he was beheaded on the 31st of January.

PRAYER 68
SAINT CYRUS

Oh Wondrous Physician, prodigious anchorite, and most glorious martyr saint Cyrus. Efficacious protector and patron of the needy. No one has come away from having asked you for a favor empty-handed. Help me, my saint, as I trustingly approach you, possessor of an ardent and fine charity towards God and a fervent devotion , so that by imitating your excellent virtues I may merit your intercession and shelter, as well as attaining the perfection that can raise me to the eternal mansions in heaven, so that in your company I may thank the Most August Trinity for the gifts that so liberally enriched your celestial spirit, Amen.

Say three Our Fathers and three Hail Marys along with one Gloria in reverence to the three attributes of Saint Cyrus as PHYSICIAN, ANCHORITE, and MARTYR. End with a Salve Regina in honor of Our Most Glorious and Blessed Mother, Mary.

STORY OF
SAINT BERNADETTE

St. Bernadette was born at Lourdes, France. Her parents were very poor and she herself was in poor health. One Thursday, February 11, 1858, when she was sent with her younger sister and a friend to gather firewood, a very beautiful Lady appeared to her above a rose bush in a grotto called Massabielle. The lovely Lady was dressed in blue and white. She smiled at Bernadette and then made the sign of the cross with a rosary of ivory and gold. Bernadette fell on her knees, took out her own rosary and began to pray the rosary. The beautiful Lady was God's Mother, the Blessed Virgin Mary. She appeared to Bernadette seventeen other times and spoke with her. She told Bernadette that she should pray sinners, do penance and have a chapel built there in her honor. Many people did not believe Bernadette when she spoke of her vision. She had to suffer much. But one day Our Lady told Bernadette to dig in the mud. As she did, a spring of water began to flow. The next day it continued to grow larger and larger. Many miracles happened when people began to use this water. When Bernadette was older, she became a nun. She was always very humble. More than anything else, she desired not to be praised. Once a nun asked her if she had temptations of pride because she was favored by the Blessed Mother. "How can I?" She answered quickly. "The Blessed Virgin chose me only because I was the most ignorant." What humility! Her feast day is April 16th.

PRAYER 69
SAINT BERNADETTE

St. Bernadette! Humble child of Lourdes, you were misunderstood and abused throughout your short life, even in religion; but through your suffering - physical, mental, spiritual - you learned to deal with the wickedness of sinners, meekly accepting your crosses and carrying them with such articulate grace. Look down upon us who continue to struggle with this mortal life, and pray that through your example we might find inner peace, hope, and faith. We ask this favor through Our Lady and Lord, with the hope of one day sharing eternity with you. Amen!

STORY OF
SAINT CLARE

Someone has said that without Saint Clare, the Franciscan movement, as we know it today, surely would not have survived. Clare gave it much energy, fought to preserve the privilege of absolute poverty, and helped keep the movement on the straight path that Saint Francis of Assisi had originally intended. Her example of love of Christ, of poverty, of self discipline and spirit of prayer have been a guiding light for centuries, for all of the Franciscan Family, for all Catholics, indeed for many not of Clare's faith.

Clare was born in Assisi in the year 1193, and nine years later moved to Perugia as a result of civil war in Assisi. In 1205 her family returned to Assisi, where she emulated her mother's love for the poor and underprivileged of Assisi.

At the age of 19, Clare heard St. Francis preaching in the Cathedral of San Rufino, next door to her home, and was so taken up with the enthusiasm and the love of Christ the Saint exhibited, that she vowed to meet with him and learn the secret of his great happiness.

In 1212, on Palm Sunday night, Clare went in secret from her house to the tiny chapel of the Porziuncula in the valley beneath the city of Assisi, and there, in candle light, surrounded the friars, St. Francis cut her beautiful hair and invested her with the garb of a Franciscan. Thus began the Second Order of Franciscans, the Poor Clares, often called the Poor Ladies of Assisi. Shortly after that, her sister, Agnes, joined Clare in religious life, much to the consternation and objection of family members.

A few weeks later, Clare and her sisters took up residence at the chapel of San Damiano, a short distance from the Porziuncula, which became their cloistered convent. The chapel of San Damiano housed the crucifix which spoke to St. Francis early in his conversion, saying: "Francis, repair my church, which you see is falling into ruin."

Clare received official permission in 1215 for the Privilege of Poverty from Cardinal Hugolino, and various other papal privileges and constitutions followed.

In 1226 Clare's own mother, Ortolona, entered the convent of Poor Ladies. That same year St. Francis died and his body was brought to San Damiano for reverence by the Sisters, on the way to burial. A year later, Pope Gregory IX (formerly Cardinal Hugolino) gave the care of the Sisters of St. Clare to the General of the Friars Minor, John Parenti.

In 1247 the rule of Innocent IV was made obligatory, and Clare began work on her own Rule of Life for the Sisters. All this time Clare suffered from severe illness, often to the point of death. But her ureides fervor never weakened. On September 16, 1252, the Rule of Clare is approved through the Cardinal Protector, Rainaldo.

On August 9, 1253, Pope Innocent IV approved the Rule of Clare with the bull "Solet Annure." The next day a friar brought the Bull of approval to Clare from Perugia, and on August 11, Clare died at her monastery of San Damiano, and was buried in the Church of San Giorgio in Assisi.

In 1255 Clare was canonized by Pope Alexander at Anagni, and in 1260 her body was transferred to the Church of Santa Chiara in Assisi.

In 1850 the coffin of St. Clare is rediscovered and twenty-two years later her body was placed in the newly erected burial chapel of Santa Chiara, where it is contained today. In 1893 the original Rule of St. Clare was found

As did St. Francis, St. Clare has continued, over the centuries to inspire countless numbers of people, ever urging them to a simple life and a deep love of the Savior. The Poor Clares continue to be visible and dramatic witnesses to that Divine Spark that enkindled the hearts of Francis and Clare, and continues to burn in the hearts of those who believe.

PRAYER 70
SAINT CLARE
SANTA CLARA

Most Glorious virgin and Most Dignified mother Saint Clare, spotless mirror of clarity and purity, most firm base of unmovable faith, fiery source of perfect charity and stronghold of all virtues.

For all those favors given to you by your most precious spouse, and for the special prerogative of having had your soul turned into a throne fit for His infinite greatness, make use of your immense piety so that He will cleanse our souls of the stains caused by

our guilt. Once our souls have been rid of all earthly fetters, we shall be worthy receptacles of His Holy Ghost. We also pray for the peace and tranquility of the Church, so that it will always be a source of unity of faith, sanctity, and good habits, all of which makes the Church unrivaled in the face of its enemies. And if what I humbly request will serve to further glorify God and strengthen my spiritual growth, then I ask that it be granted. You, my protector, please present my request to the Lord. I trust in His infinite goodness, and promise to use my boons to glorify his name. Amen, Jesus.

(It is customary to also recite the "Prayer of the Soul" after finishing this prayer.)

PRAYER 71
OUR LADY OF LOURDES

O Immaculate Virgin Mary,
Mother of Mercy,
you are the refuge of sinners,
the health of the sick,
and the comfort of the afflicted.
You know my wants,
my troubles, my sufferings.
By your appearance at the Grotto of Lourdes
you made it a privileged sanctuary
where your favors are given to people
streaming to it from the whole world.
Over the years countless sufferers
have obtained the cure for their infirmities -

whether of soul, mind, or body.
Therefore I come to you
with limitless confidence
to implore your motherly intercession.
Obtain, O loving Mother,
the grant of my requests.
Through gratitude for Your favors,
I will endeavor to imitate Your virtues,
that I may one day share in Your glory.

Amen

PRAYER 72
SAINT MARY MAGDALENE

Saint Mary Magdalene,
woman of many sins,
who by conversion
became the beloved of Jesus,
thank you for your witness
that Jesus forgives
through the miracle of love.

You, who already possess eternal happiness
in His glorious presence,
please intercede for me,
so that some day
I may share in the same everlasting joy.

Amen

PRAYER 73
ST. ALEX

Oh glorious St. Alex mine! You who have the power to chase away all that preys on the chosen of the Lord, I ask that you chase away my enemies.

Chase Satan away from me, chase liars and sorcerers away from me. Also, chase away sin and lastly, chase away all who would come to cause me harm. Get me so far from the bad ones that they'll never be able to see me. So it is.

Chase away any ill-thinking mortal. Chase away those unthinking fools who would harm me. Bring me close to the Lord so that with his divine grace he will cover me with goodness and reserve a spot for me under the shadow of the Holy Spirit, Amen, Jesus.

PRAYER 74
THE IMMACULATE CONCEPTION

O God,
who by the Immaculate Conception of
the Blessed Virgin Mary,
did prepare a worthy dwelling place for Your Son,
we beseech You that,
as by the foreseen death of this, Your Son,

You did preserve Her from all stain,
so too You would permit us,
purified through Her intercession,
to come unto You.
Through the same Lord Jesus Christ,
Your Son, who lives and reigns with You
in the unity of the Holy Spirit,
God, world without end.
Amen.

STORY OF
ST. EXPEDITUS
Feast Day: April 19th

Patron of prompt solutions, against procrastination, of speedy solutions, emergencies, avoidance of delays, financial success, merchants, navigators

Expeditus was possibly born in Armenia, at an unknown date. He was a Christian martyr, but not much else is known about him. A Parisian convent received a package from Rome containing a statue and relics of a saint, but they were unsure to whom the Holy Remains belonged. The package in which it came was marked "spedito" or "special delivery," which in Latin translates to Expeditus. Whether the relics belong to the poor Armenian martyr or the good sisters had just been duped by an ironic play on words will never really be known. The controversial statue now resides in New Orleans, and the saint's name is regularly mentioned with gratitude in the personal column of the local paper, alongside St. Jude

PRAYER 75
ST. EXPEDITUS
(EXPEDITE)

Saint Expedite, you lay in rest.
I come to you and ask that
this wish be granted.

(Name your request)

Expedite this, what I ask of you.
Expedite now this I want of you,
this very second.
Don't waste another day.
Give me what I ask for.
I know your power,
I know you because of your work.
I know you can do it.
You do this for me and I'll
spread you name with love and honor
and cause your name to be invoked.
Expedite this wish with speed, love,
honor, and goodness.
My glory to you, Saint Expedite!

(Light a candle to St. Expedite as you recite prayer
next to a glass of water for the Saint.)

Recite daily until request is granted and be sure to
give St. Expedite a gift. Also place an ad thanking
St. Expedite so that his name and fame will grow!

PRAYER 76
ANOTHER PRAYER TO
SAINT EXPEDITE

Most glorious martyr and blessed protector St. Expedite! Overlooking our demerits and based solely on your attainments and in the most precious blood of Jesus, we humbly ask that you bring us the ability to possess a humble faith, to perform abundant good works and to show fruits leading to everlasting life. Make our hope strong and unwavering, even amid toils and bitter penury. Make us have an ardent charity that each day feeds our divine love. Make us see in each other a true image of our Good God. Let our words, thoughts, and actions reflect our constant search for the glory of God; may we never stray from the teachings of our holy Mother, the Church, that we may always see in the Supreme Pastor the representative of Jesus Christ on earth; we beg you to bring us from the Lord serene, calm days for our Mother Church, fortuitous days for our country, may the sick find healing for their maladies, may the guilty find forgiveness, may the just persevere; may the infidel find the saving grace of the Holy Gospel, may those who leave this valley of tears find the joy of Christ's embrace, and may the souls of our dead find rest in everlasting peace. Finally, oh glorious martyr, make it possible for the Lord to give us the grace that we ask for in this prayer, as we confess our loyalty to Jesus here and when we reach the sweet bye and bye, Amen.

(Ask for your boon now.)

Right after this prayer, say three Our Fathers and

three special Glorias as follows: Glory be to the Father, and to the Son, and to the Holy Spirit; may they give power to St. Expedite so he may grant me what I wan fast.

PRAYER 77
Fifteen Minutes Under the Shelter of
THE SACRAMENTAL JESUS

Part 1 of 3

Most Holy Sacrament, King of Divine Justice, here I come, oh Heavenly Father, to pray for my family's health and my own, as well as the health of those dear to me. Favor me, oh Father, with good fortune in your government. Come Visit Me! Let all maleficent things stay away, sickness and obstacles, bad times and evil people, keep all of these far away from me!

Most Holy Sacrament, Divine Majesty, you who gave us life, I humbly come to beg of good fortune in my business ventures, so that I may at last free myself from loans and debts that have a stranglehold on me, promising to always help those less fortunate than myself in their hour of need, and give me, Most Holy Sacrament, PEACE!

An Apostle's Creed is now recited. This prayer is best said at 12 or 3 PM on Thursdays or Fridays, by the Holy Sacrament. Follow with the next prayer:

Part II

Blood-drenched Jesus, full of wounds and welts, let your arms and cross fall upon me so that my enemies find themselves powerless against me! Recite an Apostle's Creed to the Great Power of God now.

Part III

Triumphant Jesus , who at the cross all conquered, put an end to this pestilence, by the merits of your most Holy Mother I ask that it ends!

(Recite an Apostle's Creed and a Salve Regina.)

Exhortation: This most miraculous prayer should be carried by all, for it is known by milliard testimonies to be effective as a talisman against demons, temptations, lightning bolts, temptations, pestilence, thunder, heartaches, fevers, drownings, stalkings, sudden deaths, labor pains, fires, and other such evils and dangers. This prayer has a special quality of keeping he who carries it in the Grace of God. May The Lord make of you mercy and grant you peace! May The Lord Grant you His Holy Blessing! Amen. THIS PRAYER WAS BLESSED IN ROME, ITALY.

STORY OF
SAINT JOAN OF ARC

In French Jeanne d'Arc; by her contemporaries commonly known as la Pucelle (the Maid). She was born at Domremy in Champagne, probably on 6 January, 1412; died at Rouen, 30 May, 1431. One of five children born to Jacques d'Arc and Isabelle Romee. Shepherdess. Mystic. Received visions from Saint Margaret of Antioch, Saint Catherine of Alexandria, and Michael the Archangel from age 13.

In the early 15th century, England, in alliance with Burgundy, controlled most of what is modern France. In May 1428 Joan's visions told her to find the true king of France and help him reclaim his throne. Carrying a banner that read "Jesus, Mary", she led troops from one battle to another. Her victories from 23 February 1429 to 23 May 1430 brought Charles VII to the throne. Captured by the Burgundians and sold to the English for 10 thousand francs, she was tried by an ecclesiastical court, and executed as a heretic. In 1456 her case was retried, and Joan was acquitted (23 years too late).

PRAYER 78
SAINT JOAN OF ARC

Oh divine Joan of Arc! Humble messenger of God whose mission was to confront the great problems of your people, who were invaded by incarnate enemies. It was your heavenly mission to face the dangers of all-out war between brethren. Divine medium, inspired by spirits from God, you were chosen to liberate others. For your valor you received death at the stake, yet you were called divine by God and men alike. At your feet I ask to have the strength to overcome all the hardships of my material life. Help me have spiritual strength in order to consecrate myself for the purifying pain that cleanses the soul.

Oh Divine heroine of the mind! Pray that God not forsake me so I may live life with resignation. So be it.

This prayer is particularly good when one has lost all will to live.

TO MYTHIC PERSONAGES,
FOLK "SAINTS,"
AND
PERSONALIZED OBJECTS

Dr. Jose Gregorio Hernandez

STORY OF
DR. JOSE GREGORIO HERNANDEZ

He was born on October 26th, 1864, in Trujillo state, Venezuela. Dr. Hernandez studied medicine in Caracas and Paris, establishing a practice dedicated to helping the poor in northern Caracas. As soon as he was able, Dr. Hernandez retired from medicine and went to Italy to be a Cartusian monk. His frail health, however, kept him from taking final vows, and he died in Venezuela in 1919, while helping an invalid. Although dead only eighty-two years, he is considered well on his way to becoming am official, canonized, saint. In 1986 the Pope declared him "venerable." One of the steps towards canonization.

PRAYER 79
DR. JOSE GREGORIO HERNANDEZ

Oh merciful God who has chosen as your servant JOSE GREGORIO, who inspired by your grace practiced the most heroic virtues since he was a child, in particular demonstrating an ardent faith, an angelic purity, and a palpable sense of charity, this being the stairway that led his soul to your Divine presence, meeting you there when his earthly life came to an end. Grant us the wish to see a saintly halo over his hallowed head if by this act your honor and glory and those of your Church are magnified, we ask in the name of Jesus Christ, Amen.

(Ask Dr. Hernandez for a boon now.)

PRAYER 80
THE LUCKY HORSESHOE

By the power of the Most Holy Trinity, Lucky Horseshoe, I baptize you in the name of the Father, and of the Son, and of the Holy Ghost, bring me health, good fortune, and riches. When through the forest you wandered, Oh Lord Saint James, among the thorns and the thistles, you blindfolded your enemies with your great power. Just as you placed a horseshoe like this one on your horse's foot, and with it your horse took you to victory, I want you to invest this horseshoe with the power to grant me health, good fortune, and riches.

Jesus, I am now invoking all things holy, and wishing all things holy on this magnetic horseshoe, may it help me do whatever I want. May I be able to slip away undetected from any dangerous situation, may I achieve great power and wealth, may I make people love me, free me from all dangers and save me from my enemies and from unsafe surroundings. I believe all of this things to be real like if I were looking at them through your incomparable vision, my Lord. Amen.

PRAYER 81
THE CHUPAROSA

Oh divine hummingbird, you have the power to make my days sweeter while making my heart stronger. You take pollen from the roses and turn it into sweet nectar, so it is that you can bring me someone sweet, loving, and true. Amen.

PRAYER 82
LA MADAMA

*Oh Glorious Black Mother Whose heart is pure,
I beg of you to calm my needs and help me emerge victorious over life's challenges.*

*Teach me to survive, oh spirit called La Madama,
give me valor and give me strength, fill me with your vibration so no evil may reach me.*

*Grant me a little of your much-guarded treasure
knowing that where you are money has no value.
I implore you to accede to be my protector, Amen.*

PRAYER 83
NEGRO FELIPE

Felipe, wise slave who came from Guinea
to Venezuela by God sent and by the Virgin protected.
As a slave you proved to be a saint,
and for this you were let go.
Now I ask that you debilitate
all who would plot to have me enslaved,
my mind, body, and spirit.
Give me your blessing.
Let your wondrous luster rub off on me a little.
Keep all manner of evil away from me,
in the name of God, Amen.

(Say Three Our Fathers and Two Hail Marys.)

PRAYER 84
THE MIRACULOUS HERMANO JOSE

Benevolent and thoughtful spirit
of El Hermano Jose.
Messenger of the Almighty,
loving sentinel charged with the mission
of helping us growing wisdom and love,
we ask that you give us your support
as we face each day's decisions.
Help us, oh loving guide,
have the fortitude of character to
resist harmful thoughts and the temptation

to listen to those misguided spirits
that would induce us to err.
Illuminate our thoughts
and help us to recognize our defects,
remove the veil of ignorance from our eyes
so that we may recognize our faults.
To you, El Hermano Jose,
who we acknowledge as our guide,
and to all the other good spirits
who take an interest in our well being,
we pray that we may be worthy
of your consideration. You know our needs,
we therefore ask that you improve our lives
as we come closer to being divine, Amen.

PRAYER 85
DON PEDRITO JARAMILLO

Oh Merciful Lord who granted Don Pedrito Jaramillo the ability to heal the sick, grant that his spirit, now purified by death, be allowed to come to me in the Holy company of my Guardian Angel in order to give the strength that I need in order to regain my health. I ask also, oh Lord, that Don Pedrito's spirit reach new heights of perfection for your greater glory, oh God. Amen.

PRAYER 86
THE SPIRITS OF MONEY AND RICHES

Oh Mysterious Spirits of Money and Riches, I humbly ask that you grant my wishes. Give me silver, give me gold, and I'll share with others who are out in the cold. Amen.

PRAYER 87
FOR BEHIND THE DOOR

In the name of Almighty God I ask on his heavenly authority that when this prayer be affixed behind the main door to my home, all my enemies will be kept at bay. And all who would wish me harm will be vaporized into nothingness. For I wish no one harm and ask only for protection of my person and those of my loved ones, and I also ask that our daily bread always be forthcoming. May God bless my home.

May God keep all evil thoughts away from my mind. May God infuse my home with peace and harmony and the ability to serve as a refuge for the needy. Amen.

PRAYER 88
THE SPIRITS OF THE SEVEN HEAVENS

Oh Spirits of the Seven Heavens, hear my plea. Remove this curse cast upon me.

To the evil one who my luck does hold, send this evil back and curse him tenfold

PRAYER 89
THE SPIRIT OF FAST LUCK

Oh Spirit of Fast Luck, Oh Spirit of Good Luck, Shine on me, make my path full of success. So be it!

PRAYER 90
THE CONTROLLING SPIRITS

*Powerful Controlling Spirits,
give me the grace to hold_____down.
You I offer this candle and incense
so that nowhere can _____ hide from my control.
So be it.*

PRAYER 91
THE RED WITCH

*Oh red witch who knows my sorrow,
bring me a lover today or tomorrow.
Make me be in all his dreams,
and as he thinks of me he creams.*

PRAYER 92
THE SPIRIT OF THE MUMMY

Oh Spirit of the Mummy, Dead and Risen,
I call upon you to raise my position in business
and bring forth the results I desire.

I offer you incense and oil,
Oh Spirit of the Mummy,
to please and honor you.

Bring me what I want now.

As I will so mote it be

PRAYER 93
TAKE-AWAY PRAYER

Oh Soul of the Take-Away, I thee invoke. With thy great force take away _____ from my presence forever. Take my enemies away to the land of forgetfulness with this black candle I hereby for thee light. Oh Soul of the Take-Away, grant what I ask for I praise thee and bless thee and give thee what thou ask for, Amen.

STORY OF
THE CONGO SPIRIT

In 1844, when the Fox sisters in upstate New York ignited the Spiritualist revolution that was to sweep the North American continent and Allan Kardec began a similar movement called "Spiritism" in Europe, the spirit guides that would often manifest were American Indians, epitomizing the concept of the "noble savage." In Cuba, where Natives were exterminated by the Spaniards, the noble savage type was epitomized by African, particularly Congo, spirits. These had names such as "Jose" "Francisco" "Francisca" and "Felipe." Each practitioner had his/her own guiding Congo spirit, a custom still carried out to this day.

PRAYER 94
THE CONGO SPIRIT
Espiritu Congo

Oh glorious African spirit, by your virtues you have been rewarded with God's blessings and have been welcomed at the heavenly court to be counted among the angels and the archangels. I admire your wisdom, your kindness, and your strength. I ask you, oh Congo spirit, to deliver me from the evil intentions of those who would want to cause me harm. Bless my life, dear Congo spirit, so I may defeat my enemies, protect my home, and keep my family safe. Amen.

STORY OF
SAINT ELIJAH
SAN ELIAS, EL BARON DEL CEMENTERIO

Loa Equivalent: **Baron Samedi**   Feast Day: **July 20th.**

The loftiest and most wonderful prophet of the Old Testament. What we know of his public life is sketched in a few popular narratives enshrined, for the most part, in the First Book of Kings. These narratives, which bear the stamp of an almost contemporary age, very likely took shape in Northern Israel, and are full of the most graphic and interesting details. Every part of the prophet's life therein narrated bears out the description of the writer of Ecclesiasticus: He was "as a fire, and his word burnt like a torch "The times called for such a prophet. Under the baneful influence of his Tyrian wife Jezabel, Achab, though perhaps not intending to forsake altogether Yahveh's worship, had nevertheless erected in Samaria a temple to the Tyrian Baal (1 Kings, xvi, 32) and introduced a multitude of foreign priests (xviii 19); doubtless he had occasionally offered sacrifices to the pagan deity, and, most of all, hallowed a bloody persecution of the prophets of Yahveh.

Elijah vanished still more mysteriously than he had appeared. Like Enoch, he was "translated", so that he should not taste death. As he was conversing with his spiritual son Eliseus on the hills of Moab, "a fiery chariot, and fiery horses parted them both asunder, and Elijah went up by a whirlwind into heaven" (2 Kings 2:11)

Although St. Elijah is a Biblical prophet and a recognized saint in the Catholic Church, his identification with Baron Samedi is such that, in the context of this book, he is more mythic personage than recognized saint.

PRAYER 95
SAINT ELIJAH

Most glorious father of ours and prophet of God, Elijah; Great keeper of the Lord's honor and founder of the order of Mary of Mount Carmel, from the summit of which you saw her in prophetic vision. In that small cloud that arose from the sea, without her showing her great pains, and then she went up that holy mountain, descending upon it in the copious rains that flooded the narrow countryside of Israel, symbol of Mary's graces, which with her holy scapular she would bless the entire globe. Oh holy father of mine, Elijah, make me follow your example by dedicating my life to she who is our Mother and our comforter; make me able to walk the desert of life without fainting, fed only by the Holy Eucharist, just as you survived fed only by an ash-like bread during your flight to Mount Horeb, escaping the evil Jezebel. Teach me how to escape deceit from the world and the wiles of the Devil so that, imitating your zeal for the glory of God, I may find myself standing by you some day, singing God's praises and those of his holy Mother, who I want to see and love for all eternity. Let it be so (One Our Father and One Hail Mary are to be said at this point).

PRAYER 96
PRAYER/REVOCATION
OF ST. ELIJAH

Most powerful Saint Elijah of Mount Carmel, favored servant of the Omnipotent God; guide of us mortals who have no rudder. As I kneel on this ground before you, I seek your help in helping me rid my home of all of the evil entities that presently plague it, whether they were sent there or arrived on their own. I beg you, SAINT ELIJAH, that just as you have beaten the enemy of the person under your care, may I overcome ALL evildoers. Lend me your sword so that with it I may destroy all curses that have been brought against me and any that may be sent to me in the future.

I implore you, my saint, not to abandon me to chance when danger approaches. Help me in that hour to achieve a state of tranquility in my home; take an interest in my betterment, and do not allow a single one of my enemies to lay a hand on me.

I hereby offer to light you a candle stub each day for fifteen days, and on the fifteenth day I shall light an olive oil lamp to clear my home.

An Our Father. A Hail Mary, and a Gloria are recited here.

PRAYER 97
SAINT MARTHA THE DOMINATRIX

Oh virginal St. Martha, for the oil you will accept on this day, oil that feeds your lamp's flame, and for the cotton that was used in the ritual of Extreme Unction, I dedicate this lamp to you so you may take care of my needs and help me out of my miseries.

Help me overcome, oh Virgin, all that attacks me, just as you overcame the feral beasts that now lay at your feet. There are no obstacles you can't overcome! Give me health and work so I may take care of my needs and miseries.

Make it possible, Oh Great Mother, that _____ will be unable to live a peaceful existence until he comes to my feet. Thus, Mother, I ask by the love of God that you grant that which will diminish my sorrows, Amen Jesus.

Oh virginal St. Martha who entered the woods, scaring ferocious beasts away, tying them down with your belts, calming them down with hyssop, Oh Mother, I have no doubt that just as you broke down beasts, you can break down _____. Break him down! Break him down! Break him down!

Oh St. Martha, allow him not to sit in any chair, lie in any bed, nor have a moment of peace until surrendered at my feet he falls down. St. Martha, hear me, tend to me, by the love of God, Amen.

(Recite three Hail Marys after saying this prayer.)

108

PRAYER 98
THE JUST JUDGE
This aspect of Christ has become a mythic talisman for those evading the long arm of the law

"He who this prayer with his person brings, will never fall prey to a wasp's poisoned sting, temptations will fall by his way like old trees, and he'll never be called by the menace police. Women will bring forth their progeny finely, a man will grow old well respected and manly."

JUST JUDGE

Most Holy, Most Blessed, Most fortunate Emblem where that Just and Pious Judge died. Your mercy I seek as I ask that you make me triumph over my enemies and you free me from all demons, those who are lawmakers and slanderers also. Most Sacred Sacrament, with two I you see, with three I you tie, to the Father and the Son and the Holy Ghost. In the Garden of Desires, with the Spirit of God, to the Just Judge John spoke thus: Lord, my enemies I see approach. Let them come, for their feet are tied, their hands bound, and their eyes blinded. And as they are powerless with thee, so shall they be with me and with all those who were with you. If eyes they have, they shall not see. If hands they have, useless against thee, If mouth they have, they shan't speak to thee, and if feet they have, they'll never catch up with thee. It is Holy Mary's invincible power that covers the innocent like a loving shower. Make my enemies to a chair of pain be tied, just as the Lord to the true cross submitted. Oh my Lord, who shall I trust? The Virgin Mary I do, of course. As I trust the Most Holy Wafer. Holy Mother, clean me of sod, as you freed Jonah from a fish, for the love of God. (Recite The Apostle's Creed at this point.)

PRAYER 99
THE SPIRIT OF HATRED

Oh most holy Spirit of Hatred, heed my requests this very moment when I am mired in much pain.

I wish to be to be filled with eternal hate towards _____ may I never remember _____ May I never see _____ Again, may he disappear from my life forever more.

Oh, most Holy Spirit, make my heart feel as much hatred as astareth felt for Beelzebub so that _____'s very presence becomes hateful to me. (For better results, recite this prayer in front of image of St. Caralampius and recite five Our Fathers right after.)

PRAYER 100
INCANTATION TO
PUT DOWN A HIDDEN ENEMY

With two I thee see, with three I tie thee down whilst drinking thy blood and breaking thy heart in two. Christ rules, Christ triumphs, Christ defends us from all manner of evil. Hidden enemy, I thee defeat with the strength of St. John. I thee defeat with the sword of St. Michael, I thee torment with the help of the Lonely Soul so that not even a bad intention can thou send to me. Amen

(The Apostle's Creed is to be recited three times after each reading of the incantation.)

PRAYER 101
SAINT DESHACEDOR
SAINT UNDOER

Oh most powerful St. Undoer, judge of evildoers and greedy folk, I humble myself this day in your presence to ask that as I light this candle on the wrong side, my enemy's life goes equally wrong.

St. Undoer, glorious hero who fights evil and injustice, I beseech you, just as I've humbled myself at your feet, I want to see my enemies humbled at my feet! In the name of the Father, the Son, and of the Holy Spirit, and of the Celestial Court.

May these blessed words serve to call out my enemies so that they may fall humbled at my feet, just as Satan was humbled by St. Michael, may they have eyes that can't see, hearts that can't feel, may they be captives, may they be unable to think, may their knives not cut me, their guns not shoot me, their mouths not speak ill of me.

St. Undoer, undo in my household all that is vile, allowing goodness to flourish instead. May anyone thinking of causing me harm desist from that idea, repenting instead.

St. Undoer, saint of great might, undo any evil any enemy, actual or potential, may wish upon me. AMEN!

(Say one Our Father and one Hail Mary right after reading this prayer.)

STORY OF
THE WANDERING JEW

The Wandering Jew, also known as Ahasverus or Buttadaeus, was given the curse of immortality by Jesus Christ. As Christ was carrying his heavy cross from Pilate's hall and towards his place of crucifixion, Ahasverus, then a porter in Pilate's service and an officer of the Sanhedrim (an order of Jewish priests), struck Christ, and mocked him for walking so slowly. Christ, in turn, told the insolent porter to wait for his return, that is, until the Second Coming.

The Wandering Jew soon repented of his sins and was baptized Catholic. He grows old in the normal fashion until reaching one hundred whereupon he sheds his skin and rejuvenates to the age of thirty. The Middle Ages abound with sightings of the Wandering Jew, generally telling his story in turn for meager food and lodging, sometimes even undergoing tests of authenticity by local professors and academic figures. Encounters with the Wandering Jew occurred all throughout Europe - during the Middle Ages, there were sightings in Armenia, Poland, Moscow, and virtually every Western European city including London.

PRAYER 102
THE WANDERING JEW
(To bring someone to you)

Oh Wandering Jew known to lovers, just as you entered the Temple in Jerusalem in order to put out the most holy of flames, enter the heart of _____ and don't let him eat, nor rest, nor sleep, until he comes back to me, fully surrendered to me, body and soul.

Wandering Jew, do not allow him to sit, or lay down, or in any way rest, and let him constantly think of me and only me.

(Say three Our Fathers and three Hail Marys, and wear a Guardian Angel scapular while reading the prayer.)

PRAYER 103
THE WANDERING JEW
(To make someone wander)

Oh Wandering Jew who was cursed by Christ, just as you haven't had a day's rest, let_____ be without rest for the rest of his life, Amen.

PRAYER 104
KING MOLINERO

This powerful protective incantation dates from the 11th century.

Blessed King Molinero, sacred and pure, with the same force that you were called, I want you to call my enemies, in the name of God and the Three Divine Persons, The Father, The Son, and The Holy Ghost, with these three blessed words I want you to call my enemies so they will come humbled at the plants of my feet just as Satan came humbled to St. Michael, May the eleven thousand rays of the Sun irradiate the five senses of my enemies, submerging them just like the sponge that was offered to Jesus on the cross was submerged in vinegar and salt is submerged in water. May all bad intentions hurled at me be revoked with St. Peter's staff. And with St. Peter's keys may all senses of evil minds be opened to change to good. May their eyes not see me, their hearts not feel me. May I be free of them. May their senses not be aware of me, their feet not walk my way, their knives not hurt me, their bullets not reach me, their mouths not speak of me, with Mother Mary's loving robe may I be covered, and may I be accompanied by the Holy Sacrament to the altar.

Whoever carries this prayer with him will fear no witchcraft, nor inhuman agents, and all things from the Devil will be dominated by the following incantation: "The Holy Wafer and the Chalice I bring in my hands so that both of us can eat and the remainder will serve to honor the Word of God, the Most Holy Saint Manuel, and the Cross of Peace." Blessed and praised be God, and the Most Holy Trinity, who will condemn to Calvary all the dirty words of my enemies of both sexes at the foot of the Most Holy Cross, and with the cloth that dried Our Lord's sweat I will wipe away all bad intentions that are directed to me, and may the Holy Water that Saint John used to baptize Our Lord seal this prayer, Amen.

PRAYER 105
SAINT JOHN THE MAD
SAN JUAN LOCO

WARNING: Before you read this prayer, ask your own guardian angel for protection and guidance, and do not proceed if there is any doubt in your heart!

I ask of you who had the power to make your wife insane, to affect the five senses and seven thoughts of _____ (stomp thrice on the floor) I call upon Baal! I call upon Zeebub! I call upon Arthaklan!, St. John, infernal demons you alone control.

Send these three to_____ so that he won't be able to sit in peace, nor lay at rest, nor love a woman, be she a widow, or be she married, or single, or anything else. He won't be able to live until he comes to me!

PRAYER 106
MONEY PRAYER

Thanks to Our Lord, I lack nothing.

My purse is by God blessed, as it is ready to be opened for a needy soul as it is ready to receive bounty.

Oh God let me make wise use of my money and let me be generous with my brethren as you have instructed!

No path is closed to me, if I need anything else, or if

*I want to be richer, I look for God and He teaches me
what road to take, all I have to have is faith and be
trusting in God*

*Oh, Lord, you who have the power to fulfill the needs
of everyone, help me solve my problems and don't let
me be needing of health, wealth, and well-being. Amen*

(Recite three Our Fathers immediately afterwards.)

PRAYER 107
GET AWAY PRAYER

*Oh Spirit of the Get Away Candle ,
you have seen _____cause me strife,
make him, then, just leave my life!*

*Oh Great Spirit of great fame,
make _____forget my name!*

*I in peace just want to be,
take that bastard far from me!*

PRAYER 108
THE HOLY CROSS OF TENERIFE

May I be embraced by God the Father! May I be embraced by God the Son! May I be embraced by God the Holy Spirit! The Cross of Jerusalem is before me! Jesus Christ is who speaks for me. Halt, Lord, all who come to do me harm, make them come to my feet, May my gather be Jesus, and my godparents Saint Peter, Saint John the Baptist, and Saint James, so that the surroundings of my house may be guarded, and all that is under my care. Mother Mary and her precious Mother are my godmothers, so they may care that my body is safe from all dangers, Amen Jesus, Mary, and Joseph. Saint Helen, Saint Martha, the Lonely Soul, All the Souls of Purgatory, will free my mind of bad thoughts and will keep away all persons who would attempt against my safety.

Saint John Napomuceno, I invoke you so that you take out the tongue of whoever speaks ill of me. Saint Raphael the Archangel, I call on you to keep me healthy. Saint Francis de Paul, Our Lady of Charity, Saint Anthony and The Savior, may they guard me and keep me safe wherever I go so that no one can think ill of me. Amen Jesus, Mary, and Joseph; the Eternal Father and the Three Divine Persons guard me from anything that might affect me, so that I may come out all right from whatever my mind dictates. So that no one can get in my way. So that my businesses will always be successful, so that those who wish me bad will be tormented, and that I may realize all my plans. Amen Jesus, Mary, and Joseph.

(Say One Our Father and an Ave Maria.)

117

SPIRITIST
AND
SPIRITUALIST PRAYERS

The majority of prayers found in this section were originally channeled by French mediums in the 19th century, and compiled by the founder of Spiritism (not to be confused with Spiritualism, a similar contemporary current), Allan Kardec. Kardec's birth name was Hypolite Leon Denizard Rivail he was born on October 3, 1804, in Lyons. He was a wealthy man of letters who codified Spiritism in the middle to late 19th century. His Selected Prayers, the most important of which I am reproducing here, are some of the most popular prayers in the world. They are usually used in meetings-séances.

PRAYER 109
OPENING PRAYER

We ask the Almighty Deity to send good spirits our way while keeping at bay those who would confuse us. Give us also, oh God, the necessary light to distinguish between truth and falsehood. Give us also, oh God, the necessary light to distinguish between truth and falsehood.

Keep at bay those maleficent spirits, in the flesh or out of it, who would attempt to create discord amongst us thereby distracting us from the practice of goodness and charity towards our fellow beings. If any such spirit seeks to infiltrate this meeting, may it find no place in any of our hearts.

To you, oh benevolent spirits who have chosen to guide us, help us achieve the right frame of mind so we may humbly accept your wise counsel helping us overcome any feelings of false pride, envy, and jealousy we may harbor. Inspire us, oh spirits, to have mercy and compassion for our fellow beings, including those who would not return such feelings to us. Make it possible, oh good spirits, for us to recognize your contributions to our understanding of life and beyond by always letting us remember your benign influences.

To the mediums who will channel your teachings, oh spirits, give your blessings and make them understand the sanctity of their mission and the seriousness of the action they have agreed to undertake; give them the necessary fervor and insight to help them successfully realize their task.

If there be in this meeting anyone seeking any deleterious aim, let that person be awakened to the light of truthfulness, and let that person be forgiven for attempting to interfere with the workings of this group. We send our prayers in particular to _____, our guide, may he/she assist us and watch over us. Amen

PRAYER 110
MEDIUM'S PRAYER

We pray to Almighty God that any enlightened spirits who may be seeking our company be allowed to communicate their messages to us. Deliver us mediums from the fallacy of presuming to have "evil guides." We hope and pray that false pride will not interfere with the message that through our bodies these illuminated beings will bring. May all mediums at this meeting look upon each other as brothers and sisters, helping each other with special love and devotion.

If at any time any medium abuses the gift he or she has been granted, may the source of that power take it back to the All, for it would be better for a medium to lose his ability to channel than to use it for destructive purposes. Amen.

PRAYER 111
THE SPIRIT GUIDES

Benevolent and thoughtful spirits, messengers of the Almighty, loving sentinels charged with the mission of helping us grow in wisdom and love, we ask that you give us your support as we face each day's decisions. Help us, oh loving guides, have the fortitude of character to resist harmful thoughts and to resist the temptation to listen to the voices of evil entities who would induce us to err. Illuminate our thoughts and help us recognize our defects. Remove the veil of ignorance from our eyes so we may recognize our faults.

To you, _____, who we in particular acknowledge as our guide, and to all the other good spirits who take an interest in our well-being, we pray that we may be worthy of your consideration. You know our needs, we therefore ask that you help us improve our lives as we become closer to God. Amen

PRAYER 112
ACT OF CONTRITION

Jesus, my redeemer, pure spirit who came to this world to teach us the true doctrine of our Eternal Father, I am truly sorry for having offended you. I offer to commend myself to the observance of your Holy Commandments. I trust in your infinite goodness so you may intercede with our Merciful Father so that he may forgive my faults as he sees my true contrition and repentance, and he may give me the grace to withstand with resignation all the trials particular to this life.

Praised be the pure spirits who come from the Lord. I, a humble and backward creature, raise my thoughts and my heart in prayer so you may guide me towards the path of truth and you may light the way so I can clearly distinguish the Divine Precepts, may I never stray from them, and make me worthy of soon achieving your blessing.

I invoke your assistance in these sacred moments, so that with your divine fluids you may fortify my beleaguered incarnated spirit, with the result of comprehending and better seeing the greatness and immense Love Our Lord has for us, Amen.

PRAYER 113
KARDEC'S THANKSGIVING PRAYER

Infinitely Good God; let your name be called blessed for the goods you have given me; it would be undignified of me to attribute such graces to chance or to my own efforts.

To you, good spirits, who have served as instruments of God's will, in particular to you, my guardian angel, I thank you with all of my heart. Keep away from me the thought of being proud and any other thought not conducive to goodness. I want to thank you in particular for . . .

PRAYER 114
SPIRITIST ACT OF
SUBMISSION AND RESIGNATION

My God, you are sovereign and just; All suffering on earth must therefore have its cause and reason. I accept the motive for the affliction I have just endured as a cleansing of past faults and a trial for what's ahead.

Good spirits who protect me, give me strength to endure them without murmur. Make this experience serve to warn me and may I learn from it; may I acquire more experience; may I lose some of my pride, ambition, false vanity, and egotism, and may the whole experience serve to advance my spirituality, Amen.

PRAYER 115
TO BE SAID IN
TIMES OF IMMINENT DANGER

God Almighty; Guardian angel: HELP ME! If I am to die, May God's will be done. If I am to be saved, may I spend the rest of my life repairing what evil I have done, of which I am deeply sorry, Amen.

PRAYER 116
THANKSGIVING FOR SURVIVING IMMINENT DANGER

To you, my God, and you, my Guardian Angel, I give thanks for the aid you sent me when danger engulfed me. May the risk I took serve as a warning and may it have served as a spotlight on all of the faults that led me to it. I understand, my Lord, that my life is in your hands and that you may take it whenever you want. Inspire me through the good spirits that assist me so that I will have the good thought to employ my remaining time on this earth in worthwhile pursuits.

Custodian Angel, sustain my resolve to repair grievances others may have against me and to be a source of goodness wherever I go. In this manner, when my time comes to pass on to the spiritual realm, I shall do so less mired by imperfections, Amen.

PRAYER 117
THE CASTAWAY'S PLEA

Turn your sight towards this unworthy creature, oh God, and do not let me die among the waves of the ocean.

Give me the strength and the will to overcome the abyss, give me the grace, altogether, that your bounty does allow.

If I, like a brittle twig, thinking myself strong and

healthy, have attempted to cross the sea of humanity, in search of human delights, let me, my Lord, return to dry land, promising to be a soldier for Christ.

If I thinking myself steady, have challenged the darkness often, walking on deck while a storm rages against the boat, I promise, from now on, not to be so bold as to ignore the laments of those who suffer at sea.

And if as I follow my bliss, I've been so bold as to make fun of the lighthouse that has saved me from so many rocky arrivals, I do promise you, my Lord, never to laugh at the light that surrounds the cross where your loving son was hung.

Oh, you Father of my soul! Who listens to the afflicted, and sees my humble face ashamed of what my life used to be.

Save me, my God, please do save me! Give me enough time before death to right whatever I've wronged, do not cast away my soul!
Amen.

PRAYER 118
THANKSGIVING FOR HAVING RESISTED TEMPTATION

My God, I thank you for having permitted me to emerge victorious over evil during a recent battle I waged against temptation. Make this victory give me strength to resist future temptations; may I not fall victim to them.

And to you, my Guardian Angel, I give thanks for your assistance. May my submission to your counsel make me worthy to continue to receive it.

And to you, pure spirits from the Lord, I also offer heartfelt thanks for having helped me escape that bad road I would have taken. I hope, then, to have the good fortune of continuing to receive your protection. Amen.

PRAYER 119
NIGHTLY PRAYER

My soul is about to meet for an instance with the other spirits. May the good ones come to help me with their counsel. Guardian Angel, may I upon awakening preserve from that event a healthy and lasting impression. Permit my spirit, oh God, to meet with my loved ones who have departed, and may I receive from them spiritual fortitude and good advice. Amen.

PRAYER 120
A NEWBORN BABE
To be said by its parents

Spirit who has incarnated in the body of our baby, may you be welcome among us; God Almighty, thanks for having sent this spirit to us.

God has deposited you with us, and someday we will have to answer to God. If you belong to the new generation of spirits that must populate the earth, thank you, my God, for granting us this favor. If it is an imperfect soul, it is our duty to help it go forth the path of light by giving it right advise and right examples; if it becomes corrupted because of us, we will have to answer to God for having failed in our mission.

Lord, sustain us in our work, and give us the strength and will power to fulfill our duties. If this infant is to be tried with challenges, let it be so.

Good spirits who have come to witness this child's birth and who have been assigned to be with him for the rest of his life, do not let him down. Separate from him all imperfect spirits that would induce him to err. Give him strength to resist their temptations and give him valor to suffer with patience all the trials and tribulations that may come his way, Amen.

PRAYER 121
PRAYER OF FORGIVENESS

How many times shall I forgive my brother? I shan't forgive him seven times, but seventy times seven. Here you have a saying of Jesus' that shall call your attention and will speak highly to your heart. Look closely at these words of mercy about simple creation, so resumed and so great in its aspirations that Jesus gives his disciples, you shall always find the same thought. And he answers Peter: "You will forgive without limits, you will forgive always whatever wrongs are done to you; you will teach your brethren that forgetting of their ego which shall make them invulnerable against attacks, bad behaviors, and injuries: You shall be humble and benign of heart, never measuring your peacefulness. You will do in the end what you want the Father to do for you."

Forgive, be indulgent, charitable, and even prodigious for your age. Give because the Lord will give you; Forgive, for the Lord will forgive you; lower yourselves, for the Lord will lift you up; humble yourselves, for the Lord will have you seated at his right.

Spiritists, never forget that in word and in deed, the forgiveness of injuries must not be an empty word. If you call yourselves Spiritists, be Spiritists, then! Forget the evil that may have been done against you, and think of only one thing: The good you may do. God knows what lies inside the heart of each of us. Happy is he that can fall asleep each night saying: "I have nothing against my neighbor."

To forgive your enemies is to ask for your own forgiveness; to forgive your friends is to give them proof of your friendship; to forgive offenses is to prove you are becoming wiser; forgive, then, my friends, so God may forgive you! Amen.

PRAYER 122
PRAYER OF THE AFFLICTED

My God of Infinite Bounty; Please deign to alleviate the bitter burden of _____, if you so will.

Good Spirits, in the name of the Almighty I beg of you to help him resist his affliction. If you can do something for him, please do so. Make him understand these afflictions are necessary for his spiritual advancement. Give him faith and trust in God and in the future. In this manner, his lot will seem less heavy. Give him also strength that he not succumb to despair, for he would then loose his fruit and make his future more burdensome. Allow my thought to support him, making sure that I am helping him maintain good cheer, Amen.

PRAYER 123
THE SICK
To be said for the sick person

My God, your scrutiny is impenetrable and we know that you are allowing _____ to be sick. I beg you, Lord, to gaze upon him with compassion and deign to end his affliction.

Good Spirits, ministers of the Almighty, I beg you to second my motion to heal him. Make my prayer be like a salvific balsam poured over his sickly body and beleaguered soul.

Inspire him to be patient and submitted to the will of God, give him strength to withstand his pain with Christian resignation so he not loose the fruit of this trial to which he has been subjected.

PRAYER 124
THE SOON TO DIE

My God, I believe in you and in your boundless compassion; thus I cannot believe that you would gift man with intelligence unless it was to know you. Nor can I believe that after death there is nothing.

I believe my body to be the perishable envelope of my soul and that, once I've stopped breathing, I will awaken in the realm of the spirits.

Almighty God, I feel the fetters that bind my soul

to this body eroding. Soon I'll be giving account of my life in the body.

I will endure the results of the good and bad I may have done, for there are no illusions on the other side, no possible subterfuge. All my past will be revealed to you, and I will be judged according to my actions.

None of the wealth of this world will I take with me, honors, riches, vanity, pride, all that belongs to my body, everything material, will remain behind here on earth. Not even the smallest atom will I take from earth, nor will any of this things help me where I'm heading. I will only take with me that which belongs to my soul. Good and bad qualities that will be weighed on a rigorous balance of justice, where I'll be even more severely judged about those times when I gave up the opportunity to do good.

God of Mercy and Compassion! Let my repentance reach your heavenly presence. Do deign to extend your indulgences over my unworthy self. If it behooves you to prolong my earthly stay, then let the rest of this life be dedicated to right the wrongs I may have done.

If my hour has arrived, I take with me the comforting thought of a future life where I'll be permitted to try again to do things right, until that day when I will be privy to the joy of the elect.

If It isn't to be my lot to immediately enjoy such supreme honor, given only to the truly just, I know that such denial won't be eternal, and that sooner or later I'll get to taste the fruit of the elect, after having earned such joy.

I know my Guardian Angel and other good spirits are here, close by, ready to welcome me to the other side. Soon I'll see them just as they see me! I know I'll get to meet again with those I have loved here on earth (if I so deserve), and those I leave behind will someday be with me so that one day we will be eternally united. In the meantime, I can always come back and visit!

I know I'll meet those I've offended when I cross over to the other side, I beg for their forgiveness. Forgive my hardness of character, my pride, my injustices, and do not confuse me with shame by their presence.

I forgive all who have harmed me or have attempted to harm me, I bare no ill will towards them, and I pray that God forgives them.

Lord, give me the strength to leave behind, without regrets, the gross pleasures of this world as I enjoy the subtler pleasures of the spirit world. There, the just do not suffer torments, sufferings, or misery; only the guilty suffer there, but always with the hope of a better tomorrow.

Good Spirits and you, my Guardian Angel, make sure I do not waver in this supreme moment; make sure the refulgent light of God is reflected in my eyes thus causing a resurgence of my faith, if it be lacking. Amen.

PRAYER 125
FOR ONE WHO IS AGONIZING

Almighty and Most Merciful God. See here before you a soul leaving its earthly package to return to the realm of the spirits, its true home. May it enter there in peace and may your mercy cover its path.

Good Spirits that accompanied this soul while it traveled in the material plane, do not leave this soul which now faces a supreme change; give it strength to withstand the last pains the earth will offer it so that it can advance in the future. Inspire this soul, oh Spirits, to consecrate its repentance with its last thoughts on earth.

Direct my thoughts so that the inevitable separation will be less painful and may the comfort of hope carry its message to the departing soul, Amen.

PRAYER 126
FOR REPENTANT SPIRITS

God of mercy, you who accepts the sincere repentance of sinners, be they incarnate or not, here is in front of you a spirit that has enjoyed doing bad deeds, but is now repentant and wanting to do the right thing. Please do receive him, oh Lord, as a prodigal son, and forgive him.

Good Spirits, you've never heard his voice before, but now count him among your number, let him see the joy of those who are elected by God so he may strive to go after this joy. Sustain him in his efforts to resist the attractions of evil, and continue to reinforce his desire to be part of the world of good.

Spirit of _____, I congratulate you on your conversion and I give praise to the spirits who helped you reach this point. Amen.

PRAYER 127
FOR ONE WHO COMMITTED SUICIDE

We know, my God, what fate awaits those who disregard your laws by willfully shortening their days upon the earth. But we also know that your mercy knows no bounds: Please let your mercy flow towards the soul of _____, may our prayers and your empathy sweeten the bitter taste of the fate he is experiencing for not having had the guts to see his trials through!

Good Spirits whose mission it is to assist the downtrodden, take him under your wing, inspire him to repent from his faults v

PRAYER 128
FOR AN OBSESSED SPIRIT

Infinitely Good God, I implore you to offer the spirit who haunts _____ your mercy. Let him glimpse the Light of Heaven so he may realize the fallacy of his ways. Good Spirits, help me make him understand that by doing evil he has much to lose and by doing good, much to gain.

Spirit who derives sick pleasure from tormenting _____, hear me, for I speak in the name of God!

If you wish to reflect on what you are doing, know that you are destined to fail, for evil can never triumph over good, and you can never be stronger than God's chosen spirits.

They can keep _____ safe from you. If they haven't done so yet it is only because _____ needed to undergo a test, yet when that test is done, your influence over _____ will be a thing of the past. The evil you think you've done has only served to strengthen the person you tried to harm. Thus, your evil in the long run will have only served to condemn you.

God who is omnipotent, and his delegates the Good Spirits, who are way more powerful than you, can put an end to your obsession whenever they want and your tenacity will crash against God's Authority. But because God is so good, he wants to allow you to gain some points by ceasing in your attacks by your own free will. We are giving you the opportunity to give up your obsession on your own. If you do not give up your obsession now, you will be subjected to great punishments, you will be forced to scream for mercy. Look at your victim, who has already forgiven you, and who prays for you. This already has been having an effect in God, who is inclined to forgive you.

When you were in the flesh, wouldn't it have been stupid for you to sacrifice a fortune in order to obtain a dime? This is exactly what you are doing now as a spirit, sacrificing a great fortune of goodness for the ridiculously little pleasure derived from tormenting a soul.

See what you are missing, look how joyful the other spirits are. Stop tormenting _____ now, my friend, and let him be freed from your haunting. Join forces with the spirits of Light and allow yourself to change, for nothing is impossible for God's transforming power. Let us count you among the spirits of good, no more being part of the forces of evil, in the name of God, Amen.

PRAYER 129
THE RECENTLY DECEASED

Almighty God, may your endless mercy extend to that soul that has just passed on to the spirit realm. May your refulgent light fill his eyes with understanding. May he be surrounded with those more advanced souls who have gone before him and have learned their lessons, and may these advanced spirits teach our newly departed friend about hope and peace.

As unworthy as we may be, oh God, we dare to humbly ask you to receive our departed friend as a prodigal son, forgetting those faults that may hamper his progress in the spirit realm. Although you are the ultimate judge, Love is the ultimate quality and it is with Divine Love that we expect our friend will be received in the Great Beyond.

To you,_____, who have just left this earthly plane, I direct my most heartfelt prayers. May enlightened spirits surround you and help you shed your earthly fetters. Try to approach the Majesty of Deity. Humble yourself to God knowing his heart will find pleasure in you. Dear One! Look behind to find errors that you may never repeat them.

May you find understanding among the spirits as we who are still in the flesh pray you may continue to understand our foibles and, as we grow in the spirit, may you not forget to help those who remain behind praying for your eternal progress. Amen.

PRAYER 130
KEEP AWAY DESTRUCTIVE SPIRITS

In the powerful and holy name of Almighty God we ask that all destructive entities remain aloof from this meeting while we invoke all benevolent spirits to come to our aid. To you, destructive and evil entities who would dare to tempt us with lies, we command close our senses to you while we ask God to have mercy on our wretched souls.

To you, oh spirits who bring forth goodness and joy, help us resist the temptations evil spirits provide. Give us some your light so we may not succumb to the false shine of the evil entities. Help us not yield to false pride and strengthen our resolve to maintain ourselves clean of hatreds, jealousies, and malevolence. Let Divine Love rule our senses so no evil may enter our hearts. Amen.

PRAYER 131
FOR SUFFERING SOULS ASKING FOR PRAYERS

Kind and merciful God, may you extend your abundant mercy to include those who seek help from us, in particular_____.

Oh good and merciful spirits charged by God to instruct us, pray with us for the souls of those who would benefit from our positive thoughts. Make us vessels of Divine providence, enable us to share with the spirits of those who need light whatever light may have been granted us by that Great Spirit, the Creator of All, Amen.

PRAYER 132
DECEASED LOVED ONES

Almighty God. I ask you humbly to accept in your of Love the soul of my beloved _____, who has left behind the material plane. Make him a participant of your jubilant circle of compassion and ease his transit from the limited world of matter to the enlightenment and freedom found in the realm of the spirits. May the good spirits attend to this prayer and help my beloved reach his goal.

To you, oh_____, who I dearly loved in life, know my love follows you to the afterlife. It has been your destiny to leave me behind; help me find the strength to continue without your material presence knowing our spirits will always be together. Although the time we will spend in different realms may seem long, it is but a moment in eternity's gaze.

I thank God for allowing me the conviction of knowing you are here, blessing me with your presence, separated from me only by a thin veil. I feel your love washing over me like a tender shower of warmth. Continue to grow, beloved, knowing our love will remain intact, only becoming stronger as we both learn the path of goodness, mercy, and liberation from illusion, for in the end there is nothing but Divine Love. Peace unto your spirit till we meet again.

PRAYER 133
FOR A DECEASED ENEMY

Oh God who has seen fit to call the soul of _____ to the Great Beyond before I undertake my own inevitable journey there. I forgive him for any pain he may intentionally have caused me: May he repent of his deeds now that he no longer lives in the realm of illusion.

Keep any feelings of joy at his demise away from my weak mind, oh God, and if I in any way offended him, may he find it in his heart to forgive me as well. Amen.

PRAYER 134
FOR UNREPENTANT SOULS

Almighty God, deign to look with loving pity upon those confused souls who refuse to admit that they, as we all, have erred. Send good spirits to those souls so that with their example and, hopefully, ours, the unrepentant souls may find their way back to your goodness, beloved God.

For help in making lost and unrepentant souls find their way back to Divine Love, we invoke the name of Christ, who so discerningly dealt with wayward spirits. Help those still looking for the light, oh Jesus, find it. In the name of God we pray that unrepentant souls realize the error of their ways and humble themselves before you, God Almighty, Amen.

PRAYER 135
PRAYER OF THE SOUL

(This prayer's title is said to be due to its emanation from the subtle realm of the souls, rather than from the material plane. It relieves symptoms of mental illnesses caused by other than natural causes.)

My God, please forgive the particular soul wandering through the fog of ignorance which has attached itself to me. My Father, light the way for this soul to travel. Kindred soul wasting much precious time, heed my voice

142

as I have nothing but your progress in mind. You who are attached to my material being, It is my wish that you detach yourself from me. God my Father, I ask that you give this soul an atom of understanding so he may let go of my being. I also ask for your forgiveness, oh God, if in any way I have offended this confused soul who has so perniciously attached himself to me.

I want this soul to realize that it is a spirit being, no longer encased in the flesh. Oh, spirit brother, realize that you are a spirit! Search out those beings who can help you on the other side. From this moment onward you must think in a very different manner! It is my wish that your guide will enlighten your way. My God, if this soul has harbored evil intentions against me, I beg of you to forgive him! Brother, I will pray three Our Fathers each day for nine days to help you achieve light in the great beyond, Amen.

PRAYERS FOR
SPECIFIC OUTCOMES

PRAYER 136
PRAYER FOR PEACE

O Lord Jesus Christ, Who said to Your Apostles: "Peace I leave with you, My peace I give to you," regard not my sins but the faith of Your People, and deign to give them peace and unity according to Your Will: Who live and reign, God, world without end. Amen.

PRAYER 137
AGAINST DEMONIC SNARES

LORD JESUS Christ, the Son of God, having struck down the ancient serpent and bound him in Tartarus by bonds of darkness, protect me from his snares. Through the prayers of our Most Holy Lady, the Theotokos and Ever-virgin Mary, of the holy Archangel Michael and all the Heavenly hosts, of the holy Prophet and Baptist John, of the holy Evangelist John the Theologian, of the holy Martyr Cyprian and the Martyr Justinia, of St. Nicholas the wonderworker, of St. Nikita of Novgorod, of St. John of Shanghai and San Francisco, the wonderworker ... and of all the saints, by the power of the life-giving Cross and by the intercession of my Guardian Angel, deliver me from evil spirits, from cunning people, from sorcery, curses, the evil eye, and from any slanders of the enemy. By Thine almighty power preserve me from evil, so that I, enlightened by Thy light, may safely reach the quiet anchorage of the Heavenly Kingdom and there eternally thank Thee, my Savior, together with Thine unoriginate Father and Thy Most Holy and Life-giving Spirit. Amen

PRAYER 138
TO BE SAID BEFORE
A JUDGE PASSES SENTENCE

Omnipotent God; Supreme Justice; Infinite Bounty. At this critical junction, when sentence is about to be imposed on me, because as a mortal man condemned to err and commit crimes because of the circumstances of my life, I prostrate myself in front of you, the weight of my faults on my shoulders. I beg for clemency, Oh Lord, and the help of all good spirits, so that I may be helped in this such difficult hour of my life, where my freedom may be impaired by this outdated form of punitive sentence I face.

Oh my God! If in this world we live in brother shall judge brother, because the law of men imposes on men this duty, you can influence all outcomes so that my sentence is minimal. My soul hurts, my God, it knows that the man who judges the accused is his brother, and if I am to suffer my brother's judgment, my God, let it be you who influences his decision as you see my heart and soul inflamed with repentance and shame, ready to turn a new leaf, one dedicated to your service.

Oh Good spirits, my Guardian Angel, do not abandon me. Influence the judge so my sentence is minimal, and if I have to serve some time, make that time less onerous, my God. And I pray for the day when it shall be God who judges us in the promised land, under his just sentencing we shall all realize the bliss of our hearts. Amen.

PRAYER 139
FOR EMPLOYMENT

God, our Father, I turn to you seeking your divine help and guidance as I look for suitable employment. I need your wisdom to guide my footsteps along the right path, and to lead me to find the proper things to say and do in this quest. I wish to use the gifts and talents you have given me, but I need the opportunity to do so with gainful employment. Do not abandon me, dear Father, in this search, but rather grant me this favor I seek so that I may return to you with praise and thanksgiving for your gracious assistance. Grant this through Christ, our Lord. Amen

PRAYER 140
FOR LIFE

O God, our Creator, all life is in your hands from conception until death. Help us to cherish our children and to reverence the awesome privilege of our share in creation. May all people live and die in dignity and love. Bless all those who defend the rights of the unborn, the handicapped and the aged. Enlighten and be merciful toward those who fail to love, and give them peace. Let freedom be tempered by responsibility, integrity and morality. Amen.

PRAYER 141
FOR THE SICK

Father of goodness and love, hear our prayers for the sick members of our community and for all who are in need. Amid mental and physical suffering may they find consolation in your healing presence. Show your mercy as you close wounds, cure illness, make broken bodies whole and free downcast spirits. May these special people find lasting health and deliverance, and so join us in thanking you for all your gifts. We ask this through the Lord Jesus who healed those who believed. Amen

PRAYER 142
FOR A HAPPY DEATH

O God, great and omnipotent judge of the living and the dead, we are to appear before you after this short life to render an account of our works. Give us the grace to prepare for our last hour by a devout and holy life, and protect us against a sudden and unprovided death. Let us remember our frailty and mortality, that we may always live in the ways of your commandments. Teach us to "watch and pray" (Lk 21:36), that when your summons comes for our departure from this world, we may go forth to meet you, experience a merciful judgment, and rejoice in everlasting happiness. We ask this through Christ our Lord. Amen.

PRAYER 143
FOR PERSONAL FORGIVENESS

Lord Jesus, I am sorry for my sins, I renounce Satan and all his works, And I give you my life. I accept you whom I've just received in communion. I now receive and accept you as my personal Lord and my personal Savior, and as we just prayed, fill us with Your Holy Spirit. Amen.

PRAYER 144
TO SEPARATE TWO PEOPLE

I offer and invoke this prayer to the Spirit of Hatred to the Guardian Angel of _____ and _____, so that he infuses both parties with hate and separation and let each person experience loathing for the other each time each thinks of the other. May the aromas that once meant something to _____.

And _____ now bring only revulsion to them. May the moments they shared bring only bad memories. May they ignore each other if they happen to meet. May they not understand each other if they happen to speak. I call upon the Spirit of the Road so that _____ and _____ will never walk the same path again. Amen.

FOUNDATION
PRAYERS

These classic Christian prayers
are often used as foundations upon which other,
more specific prayers are built.

PRAYER 145
THE OUR FATHER
Also known as The Lord's Prayer

One of the most beautiful and revered prayers ever made, it was taught by JESUS CHRIST himself to his disciples.

Our Father who art in heaven,
hallowed be thy name,
thy kingdom come,
thy will be done,
on earth, as it is in heaven,
give us this day,
our daily bread,
and forgive us our trespasses,
as we forgive those,
who trespass against us
and lead us not into temptation,
but deliver us from evil.   Amen.

PRAYER 146
23rd PSALM

Revered by Christians and Jews alike, attributed to the pen of David, this prayer has helped millions of souls.

The Lord is my shepherd; I shall not want.
He maketh me to lie down in green pastures; He leadeth
me beside still waters.
He restoreth my soul;
He leadeth me in the paths of

righteousness for His name's sake.
Yea, though I walk through the valley
of the shadow of death,
I will fear no evil;
for thou art with me.
Thy rod and thy staff they comfort me.
Thou preparest a table before
me in the presence of mine enemies;
Thou anointest my head with oil;
my cup runneth over.
Surely goodness and mercy shall
follow me all the days of my life;
and I will dwell in the house of
the Lord forever.

PRAYER 147
THE MAGNIFICAT

For thousands of years, Christian Gnostics, "kabbalists" and magicians have used this beautiful hymn authored by Mary, mother of Jesus, in surprising ways. "Carry it with you and you'll be protected, recite it before you commit an indecent act, and you will be forgiven." A 16th century grimoire said.

My soul magnifies the Lord,
And my spirit rejoices in God my Savior.
For He has regarded the low estate of His handmaiden,
For behold, henceforth all generations shall call me blessed.
For He who is mighty has done great things for me, and holy
is His name. And His mercy is on those who fear Him from
generation to generation.

He has shown strength with His arm:
He has scattered the proud in the imagination of their hearts.
He has put down the mighty from their thrones,
and exalted those of low degree.
He has filled the hungry with good things;
and the rich He has sent empty away.
He has helped His servant Israel, in remembrance of His mercy;
As He spoke to our fathers, to Abraham and to His posterity forever.

Glory be to the Father and to the Son and to the Holy Spirit. As it was in the beginning, is now and ever shall be, world without end. Amen.

PRAYER 148
SALVE REGINA

Hail, Holy Queen, mother of mercy, our life, our sweetness and our hope.

To thee do we cry, poor banished children of Eve.

To thee do we send up our sighs, mourning and weeping in this valley of tears.

Turn then, most gracious advocate, thine eyes of mercy toward us, and after this, our exile, show unto us the blessed fruit of thy womb, Jesus.

O clement, O loving, O sweet Virgin Mary.
V. Pray for us, O holy mother of God:
R. That we may be made worthy of the promises of Christ.

Let us pray:
Almighty and everlasting God, by the cooperation of the Holy Spirit thou hast prepared the body and soul of Mary, glorious Virgin and Mother, to become the worthy habitation of Thy Son; Grant that by her gracious intercession, in whose commemoration we rejoice, we may be delivered from present evils and from everlasting death. Through the same Christ our Lord. Amen.

V. May divine assistance remain with us always.
R. Amen.

PRAYER 149
HAIL MARY

Hail Mary full of Grace, the Lord is with thee. Blessed are thou among women and blessed is the fruit of thy womb Jesus. Holy Mary Mother of God, pray for us sinners now and at the hour of our death Amen.

PRAYER 150
GLORIA

Glory be to the Father and to the Son and to the Holy Spirit. As it was in the beginning is now, and ever shall be, world without end. Amen.

PRAYER 151
THE APOSTLES' CREED

Said to have been composed by the twelve apostles on the day of Pentecost, each apostle contributing an article.

(1) *I believe in God the Father Almighty;*
And in Jesus Christ, His only Son, our Lord;

(2) *Who was conceived by the Holy Ghost, born of the Virgin Mary;*

(3) *Suffered under Pontius Pilate, was crucified, dead, and buried;*

(4) *He descended into hell; the third day He rose again from the dead;*

(5) *He ascended into Heaven, where he sits at the right hand of God the Father Almighty;*

(6) *From thence He shall come to judge the living and the dead.*

(7) *I believe in the Holy Ghost;*

(8) *The Holy Catholic Church, the communion of saints*

(9) *The forgiveness of sins,*

(10) *The resurrection of the body, and*

(11) *Life everlasting.*

(12) *Amen.*

PRAYER 152
THE SIGN OF THE CROSS

By the sign of the Holy Cross
From our enemies deliver us
Lord Our God
In the name of the Father,
The Son,
And the Holy Spirit.
Amen.

DEVOTIONAL
PRAYERS

PRAYER 153
MORNING PRAYER

In the name of our Lord Jesus Christ I will begin this day. I thank you, Lord, for having preserved me during the night. I will do my best to make all I do today pleasing to You and in accordance with Your will. My dear mother Mary, watch over me this day. My Guardian Angel, take care of me. St. Joseph and all you saints of God, pray for me... (Followed by Daily Offering)

PRAYER 154
DAILY OFFERING

O Jesus, through the immaculate heart of Mary, I offer you my prayers, works, joys and sufferings of this day in union with the holy sacrifice of the Mass throughout the world. I offer them for all the intentions of your sacred heart: the salvation of souls, reparation for sin, the reunion of all Christians. I offer them for the intentions of our bishops and of all the apostles of prayer, Amen.

PRAYER 155
EVENING PRAYER

O my God, at the end of this day I thank You most heartily for all the graces I have received from You. I am sorry that I have not made a better use of them. I am sorry for all the sins I have committed against You. Forgive me, O my God, and graciously protect me this night. Blessed Virgin Mary, my dear heavenly mother, take me under your protection. St. Joseph, my dear Guardian Angel, and all you saints of God, pray for me. Sweet Jesus, have pity on all poor sinners, and save them from hell. Have mercy on the suffering souls in purgatory... (Followed by an Act of Contrition)

PRAYER 156
CATHOLIC ACT OF CONTRITION

O my God, I am heartily sorry for having offended You and I detest all my sins, because I dread the loss of heaven and the pains of hell, but most of all because they offend you, my God, who are all good and deserving of all my love. I firmly resolve, with the help of your grace, to confess my sins, to do penance and to amend my life.

PRAYER 157
PRAYER BEFORE MEALS

Bless us Oh Lord, and these thy gifts, which we are about to receive, from thy bounty, through Christ, Our Lord. Amen.

PRAYER 158
EVENING PRAYER

Now that the day has come to a close, I thank you, O Lord, and entreat that the evening with the night may be without sin, grant this to me, O Savior, and save me.

Glory be to the Father and to the Son and to the Holy Spirit. Now that the day has passed, I glorify you, O Master, and entreat that the evening with the night may be without offence; grant this to me, O Savior, and save me.   Now and always, and forever and ever. Amen

PRAYER 159
ANOTHER EVENING PRAYER

Now that the day has run its course, I praise you, O Holy One, and entreat that the evening with the night may be undisturbed, grant this to me, O Savior, and save me.

PRAYER 160
WICCAN EVENING PRAYER

Lord and Lady, twirl about.
Guide me day and night, throughout.
Guide me through each passing hour
And grant me Your protective power.
From head to toe, from sky to ground,
Keep me safe and well and sound.

PRAYER 161
ANIMA CHRISTI

Soul of Christ, make me holy. Body of Christ, save me. Blood of Christ, fill me with love. Water from Christ's side, wash me. Passion of Christ, strengthen me. Good Jesus, hear me. Within your wounds, hide me. Never let me be parted from you. From the evil enemy, protect me. At the hour of my death, call me. And tell me to come to you. That with your saints I may praise you. Through all eternity. Amen.

PRAYER 162
GUARDIAN ANGEL PRAYER

O Holy Angel, attendant of my wretched soul and of mine afflicted life, forsake me not, a sinner, neither depart from me for mine inconstancy. Give no place to the evil demon to subdue me with the oppression of this mortal body; but take me by my wretched and outstretched hand, and lead me in the way of salvation. Yea, O holy Angel of God, the guardian and protector of my hapless soul and body, forgive me all things whatsoever wherewith I have troubled thee, all the days of my life, and if I have sinned in anything this day. Shelter me in this present night, and keep me from every affront of the enemy, lest I anger God by any sin; and intercede with the Lord in my behalf, that He might strengthen me in the fear of Him, and make me a worthy servant of His goodness. Amen.

PRAYER 163
PRAYER TO OUR LADY

Remember, O most loving Virgin Mary, that never was it known that anyone who fled to your protection, implored your help, or sought your intercession was left unaided. Inspired with this confidence, we turn to you, O Virgins of virgins, our Mother. To you we come, before you we stand, sinful and sorrowful. O Mother of the Word Incarnate, do not despise our petitions, but in your mercy hear us and answer us. Amen.

PRAYER 164
TO THE HOLY SPIRIT

Breathe into me Holy Spirit, That all my thoughts may be holy. Move in me, Holy Spirit, that my work, too, may be holy. Attract my heart, Holy Spirit, that I may love only what is holy. Strengthen me, Holy Spirit, that I may defend all that is holy. Protect me, Holy Spirit, that I always may be holy.

PRAYER 165
TO THE HOLY SPIRIT (2)

Spirit of wisdom and understanding, enlighten our minds to perceive the mysteries of the universe in relation to eternity. Spirit of right judgment and courage, guide us and make us firm in our baptismal decision to follow Jesus' way of love. Spirit of knowledge and reverence, help us to see the lasting value of justice and mercy in our everyday dealings with one another. May we respect life as we work to solve problems of family and nation, economy and ecology. Spirit of God, spark our faith, hope and love into new action each day. Fill our lives with wonder and awe in your presence which penetrates all creation. Amen.

PRAYER 166
THE DIVINE PRAISES

Blessed be God. Blessed be His Holy Name. Blessed be Jesus Christ, true God and true Man. Blessed be the Name of Jesus. Blessed be His Most Sacred Heart. Blessed be Jesus in the Most Holy Sacrament of the Altar. Blessed be the great Mother of God, Mary most Holy. Blessed be her Holy and Immaculate Conception. Blessed be her Glorious Assumption. Blessed be the Name of Mary, Virgin and Mother. Blessed be St. Joseph, her most chaste spouse. Blessed be God in His Angels and in His Saints

PRAYER 167
THE UNIVERSAL PRAYER
(Attributed to Pope Clement XI)

Lord, I believe in you: increase my faith.
I trust in you: strengthen my trust.
I love you: let me love you more and more.
I am sorry for my sins: deepen my sorrow.

I worship you as my first beginning,
I long for you as my last end,
I praise you as my constant helper,
And call on you as my loving protector.

Guide me by your wisdom,
Correct me with your justice,
Comfort me with your mercy,

Protect me with your power.

I offer you, Lord, my thoughts: to be fixed on you;
My words: to have you for their theme;
My actions: to reflect my love for you;
My sufferings: to be endured for your greater glory.

I want to do what you ask of me:
In the way you ask,
For as long as you ask,
Because you ask it.

Lord, enlighten my understanding,
Strengthen my will,
Purify my heart,
and make me holy.

Help me to repent of my past sins
And to resist temptation in the future.
Help me to rise above my human weaknesses
And to grow stronger as a Christian.

Let me love you, my Lord and my God,
And see myself as I really am:
A pilgrim in this world,
A Christian called to respect and love
All whose lives I touch,
Those under my authority,
My friends and my enemies.

Help me to conquer anger with gentleness,
Greed by generosity,
Apathy by fervor.
Help me to forget myself
And reach out toward others.

Make me prudent in planning,
Courageous in taking risks.
Make me patient in suffering, unassuming in
prosperity.

Keep me, Lord, attentive at prayer,
Temperate in food and drink,
Diligent in my work,
Firm in my good intentions.

Let my conscience be clear,
My conduct without fault,
My speech blameless,
My life well-ordered.
Put me on guard against my human weaknesses.
Let me cherish your love for me,
Keep your law,
And come at last to your salvation.

Teach me to realize that this world is passing,
That my true future is the happiness of heaven,
That life on earth is short,
And the life to come eternal.

Help me to prepare for death
With a proper fear of judgment,
But a greater trust in your goodness.
Lead me safely through death
To the endless joy of heaven.
Grant this through Christ our Lord. Amen.

PRAYER 168
PRAYER OF SELF-DEDICATION

Take O Lord, and receive my entire liberty, my memory, my understanding and my whole will. All that I am and all that I possess You have given me: I surrender it all to You to be disposed of according to Your will. Give me only Your love and Your grace; with these I will be rich enough, and will desire nothing more. Amen

PRAYER 169
FOR AMERICA

Father, we beg Your blessing for the Right to Life, the Unborn, the weak, the sick and the old; all who are finding themselves being targets of the vicious culture of death; that our Lord Jesus bless and protect all who stand up for the Christian dignity of persons. That God enlighten those who are traveling down death's highway by their involvement, in any way, with either the contemporary death culture, selfism, relativism, or any of the new age errors of our times, that God envelop our culture with His Divine protection and help us both individually and as a nation to true enlightenment, conversion and repentance of our selves and our culture. Help us to turn from our lack of respect for the sanctity of Life, and return to, and once again become a Christian nation, on the narrow road, that is, the path to becoming a nation and culture, under God. Amen.

PRAYER 170
SERENITY PRAYER

God grant me the serenity to accept the things I cannot change;
courage to change the things I can; and wisdom to know the difference.

STORY OF
THE JESUS PRAYER

Contrary to popular belief, Christianity does not lack the power of the mantra. While it is obvious that Hinduism and Buddhism have continued to make use of spoken protective mantras much more successfully than traditions stemming from Abraham—Judaism, Christianity, and Islam—One powerful Christian incantation has survived in the Byzantine rite of the Catholic Church, it is called The Jesus Prayer, and as its mystic power is being rediscovered in the West, it is becoming more and more popular. The Jesus prayer is the only ancient Christian prayer left that asks that you synchronize your breathing with the invocation of the name of Jesus. In this prayer, you do not have to occupy your thoughts with the content of the prayer (as you would do with a rosary); you are provided with a point of attention which frees your mind to receive the vibratory frequencies of the healing name of Jesus. The result is that the prayer serves to strengthen and protect you at a "not-conscious" level.

This powerful invocation has its roots not only in the New Testament, but even further back in the Old Testament, where we see a developed personal conviction that the invocation of the name of God brings with it the conscious realization of His presence: "Call on my name, I will hear" (Zec. 13: 9). Once a year, on the day of Atonement, Yahweh's name was pronounced only by the high priest who was chosen to offer sacrifice inside the "Holy of Holies" of the temple in Jerusalem. In the New Testament, there is ample evidence of the power that emanates from the reverent pronouncing of the name of Jesus. Philippians 2:9-10 tells us that "God has given Him a name that is above all names so that at the name of Jesus every knee shall bend in heaven, on earth, and under the earth." Lost in the beginnings of Christianity, the Jesus Prayer became a powerful mantra when executed as follows. After taking a deep breath, you say: LORD, JESUS CHRIST. Then, after softly exhaling, you say: SON OF GOD. Again, you take a deep breath and say, HAVE MERCY ON ME. Then you exhale and say A SINNER. On a set of beads designed for this purpose, called "Jesus beads," you count the times you say the prayer, which gives you more power the more times you repeat it. Notice that you are inhaling, TAKING IN, the Holy Name, while exhaling, THROWING OUT, your own sinful nature. This simple exercise allows angelic, high vibrations to permeate your being while expelling negative, low vibrations sent to you by a psychic attacker.

PRAYER 171
THE JESUS PRAYER

Lord Jesus Christ
Son of God
Have mercy on me
A sinner.

You can also write the prayer on parchment using dragon's blood ink, place parchment on a red flannel bag, dress with sacramental oil or holy water, and keep with you at all times for constant protection.

CLOSING NOTES

WHAT TO PRAY FOR?
FORMULA FOR SUCCESSFUL PRAYER

To the ignorant and the uninitiated this may sound like a foolish question. But those of us who know the uses, to which prayer can be put, know differently. The fool comes to God with a fool's questions. He may feel that he is entitled to ask for anything. Of course he is entitled to ask. But by the same token, God is not compelled to grant the request.

The First Injunction:
"Know What to Pray For."

The first important thing to do is make certain just what it is that we want. Someone once said that there were only two tragedies in life. One was not getting what we want, the other, getting it! Sometimes we wish, hope, strive and even pray for things that will do us more harm than good. We have not thought sufficiently on the subject of our desire.

The Second Injunction:
"Pray Only For Good."

The second important thing to remember is what we should not pray for something that is going to harm another. And that goes for no matter whom the somebody else happens to be. There are no enemies in our life. We are our own first and worst enemy. We must learn to conquer ourselves. The Good Book tells us that, *"He who conquers himself is greater than he who conquers a city"*. Hence we must first of all be masters ourselves. God is not here to help us wreak vengeance on any person. We should pray for people, not against them.

The cross, the hex, the evil eye, the curse of malediction are the properties of the devil, and have no place in our dealing with God. We all know the familiar story of the person who prayed for vengeance. He asked that a terrible curse be placed on another. This person prayed regularly and fervently that some misfortune be visited on another. That was the only aim in his life. By a strange and ironical twist of fate, the very misfortune that he wished on the head of another, fell on his own life. So he was repaid for his prayer. Had this person used the same time, effort and energy on intelligently applied prayer, he might have been able to reap the benefits that God gives to them who put their trust in Him and in Him alone.

The Third Injunction: "Pray For The Things That Are Yours."

The third important thing to remember is to pray for something that fits into our life. Something that we are prepared for, something that should belong to us. For example: It would be folly for each of us to ask God to make us the President of the United States. To begin with, very few people are prepared or equipped to be President, and there can be but one President at a time. Other people pray for a million dollars. What they should really pray for is the opportunity to work, and earn a fair salary.

We must pray for those things that are within our reach, things that fit into our lives. Those things that we are prepared to accept and accomplish. As we progress in our studies, we become more expert in our contacts with God. We build up our receptiveness. As the fruits of our prayers come to us, we are prepared. When the time comes, we understand and appreciate the blessings that our sincere prayers are sure to bring us. God gives us a sign to show us that He has heard our prayers. It is up to us to discover the way in which God has worked His wonder to perform. Our growth and development control our ability to recognize these signs.

The Fourth Injunction:
"Raise Your Voice In Prayer For Those Who Are Near You and Those Who Call You, Friend."

The fourth important thing to bear in mind is that we can pray for another. Very often our lives are so intimately tied up with the life of another, that the sympathetic bond becomes a real spiritual bond.

There are people whose lives influence one another. It may be man and wife, lovers, parent and child, friends, or it may be any two people whose understanding sympathy makes them, to all spiritual intents and purposes, one. These people are usually ones who have developed the spiritual understanding to such a degree that they can keep their prayers within the limits that understanding prayer demands.

Some people have developed their receptiveness to so high a degree that they can influence the lives of others in a beneficial way. They are the High Chosen Few. Those whose lives and efforts have attained so high a spiritual plane that their saintliness shines from them like a nimbus or a halo of light. They are the True Priests of Life. They understand the physical and spiritual limitations of others. Knowing and understanding these limitations, they know how to help with their prayers.

In matters of deep despondency and sadness, in matters of illness and health, we can pray for help for those whom we love, or those who are near to us. God understands these prayers. He knows that they are unselfish prayers, and is ready to accept them as such.

We must be as ready to give thanks, as we are to ask a favor. God measures our capacity for blessings by our ability to appreciate those things that we have.

We must learn to be thankful for small favors.

We must always be ready and willing to admit that we have been in error. That we were not prepared for the blessings that sincere Prayer brought to us, if we overlooked the opportunities to serve. There should be no shame in facing God and telling Him that we have erred. That's why we are human beings. We must at all times be ready to forgive those who have trespassed against us. We should ask God to forgive them. Have we not a most beautiful example of forgiveness before us?

Remember how He said, in the midst of His travail:

"Forgive them, Father, for they know not what they do."

That should be our motto in Prayer. For that moment when we can understandingly forgive others, that moment, we have made our most intimate contact with the Lord and Master.

Above all, we must be open and above board with our God. Never try to make excuses for anything that you've done. God knows your intention before you yourself have thought of it.

Hence we learn the answer to our Question "What to Pray For".

PRAY FOR THE VISION TO SEE GOD'S WORKS.

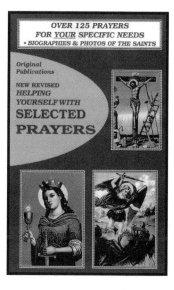

ITEM #214
$7.95

HELPING YOURSELF WITH SELECTED PRAYERS

NOW OVER *120,000* IN PRINT!

The New Revised Helping Yourself with Selected Prayers provides an English translation for over 125 prayers of various religious beliefs. These prayers will provide a foundation upon which you can build your faith and beliefs. It is through this faith that your prayers will be fulfilled.

An index is provided to help the reader find the appropriate prayer for his or her particular request. The index also includes suggestions regarding the appropriate candle to burn while saying a particular prayer.

The devotions within these pages will help you pray consciously, vigorously, sincerely and honestly. True prayer can only come from within yourself.

ISBN 0-942272-01-3 5½"x 8½" 112 pages $7.95

Revised and Expanded

Success and Power
Through Psalms

By Donna Rose

For thousands of years, men and women have found in the Psalms the perfect prayer book, possessing wisdom applicable to every human situation. Wise men and women of deep mystical insight have also learned to decipher the magical formulas David and the other Psalmists hid behind the written words. These formulas help the seeker solve everyday problems, achieve higher states of consciousness, gain material and spiritual wealth, as well as help defend himself or herself against psychic attacks and all manner of dangers.

The Revised and Expanded edition of Donna Rose's classic offers over 300 simple to perform magical rituals to help you manifest all of your desires using the magical powers of the psalms.

ISBN 0-942272-79-X 5½"x 8½ $5.95

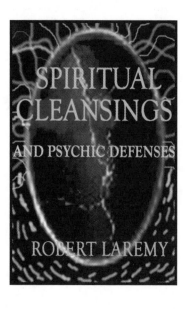

ITEM #238
$8.95

SPIRITUAL CLEANSINGS & PSYCHIC DEFENSES

BY ROBERT LAREMY

Psychic attacks are real and their effects can be devastating to the victim. Negative vibrations can be as harmful as bacteria, germs and viruses. There are time-honored methods of fighting these insidious and pernicious agents of distress. These techniques are described in this book and they can be applied by you. No special training or supernatural powers are needed to successfully employ these remedies. All of the procedures described in this book are safe and effective, follow the instructions without the slightest deviation. The cleansings provided are intended as *"over-the-counter"* prescriptions to be used by anyone being victimized by these agents of chaos.

ISBN 0-942272-72-2 5½"x 8½" 112 pages $8.95

New Revised

The Master Book of Candle Burning

How to Burn Candles for Every Purpose

POWERFUL
PSALM
RITUALS

HENRI GAMACHE

#043
$7.95

"How can I burn candles in a manner which will bring me the most satisfaction and consolation?"

In order to answer that question it is necessary to eliminate all technical, dry and often times torturous historical background. It is necessary to sift and sort every fact, scrutinize every detail, search for the kernel.

It is to be hoped that this volume answers that question in a manner which is satisfactory to the reader. It has been necessary, of course, to include some historical data and other anthropological data in order to better illustrate the symbolism involved in modern candle burning as practiced by so many people today.

This data has been accumulated from many sources: it has been culled from literally hundreds of books and articles. The modern rituals outlined here are based upon practices which have been described by mediums, spiritual advisors, evangelists, religious interpreters and others who should be in a position to know.

It has been the author's desire to interpret and explain the basic symbolism involved in a few typical exercises so that the reader may recognize this symbolism and proceed to develop his own symbolism in accordance with the great beauty and highest ethics of the Art.

ISBN 0-942272-56-0   5½"x 8½" $7.95

ORIGINAL PUBLICATIONS   TOLL FREE: 1-888-622-8581

#163
$9.95

THE NEW REVISED
6ᵀᴴ & 7ᵀᴴ
BOOKS OF MOSES
AND THE
MAGICAL USES OF THE PSALMS

EDITED BY MIGENE GONZALEZ WIPPLER

This revised edition is an attempt at the reorganization of a work, long hailed by occult masters as a valuable tool in the study and practice of cabalistic magic.

It is hoped that this new edition will make the teachings of this venerable work attainable to many readers who up to now were unable to understand it.

ISBN 0-942272-02-1   5½"x 8½ $9.95

ITEM #172
$8.95

HELPING YOURSELF WITH
MAGICKAL OILS A-Z
By Maria Solomon

The most thorough and comprehensive
workbook available on the

Magickal Powers of Over 1000 Oils!

Easy to follow step-by-step instructions
*for more than 1500
Spells, Recipes and Rituals for*
Love, Money, Luck, Protection
and much more!

ISBN 0-942272-49-8 5½"x 8½" $8.95

ORIGINAL PUBLICATIONS

- ☐ **HELPING YOURSELF WITH SELECTED PRAYERS;** *Volume 1*; $7.95
- ☐ **HELPING YOURSELF WITH SELECTED PRAYERS:** *Volume 2*; $9.95
- ☐ **UNHEXING AND JINX REMOVING;** by Donna Rose - $5.95
- ☐ **SUCCESS AND POWER THROUGH PSALMS;** by Donna Rose - $5.95
- ☐ **MAGICAL RITUALS FOR MONEY;** by Donna Rose - $5.95
- ☐ **MAGICAL RITUALS FOR LOVE;** by Donna Rose - $5.95
- ☐ **DREAM YOUR LUCKY LOTTERY NUMBERS;** Canizares $5.95
- ☐ **PSALM WORKBOOK:** Robert Laremy - $7.95
- ☐ **SPIRITUAL CLEANSINGS & PSYCHIC PROTECTION;** Robert Laremy $8.95
- ☐ **NEW REVISED MASTER BOOK OF CANDLEBURNING;** Gamache - $7.95
- ☐ **THE MAGIC CANDLE;** Charmaine Dey $6.95
- ☐ **NEW REV. 6&7 BKS. OF MOSES;** Wippler $9.95
- ☐ **MYSTERY OF THE LONG LOST 8,9,10TH BOOKS OF MOSES;** Gamache - $7.95
- ☐ **VOODOO & HOODOO;** by Jim Haskins - $16.95
- ☐ **COMPLETE BOOK OF VOODOO;** Robert Pelton $16.95
- ☐ **VOODOO CHARMS AND TALISMANS;** Robert Pelton $9.95
- ☐ **PAPA JIM'S HERBAL MAGIC WORKBOOK;** Papa Jim - $7.95
- ☐ **HELPING YOURSELF WITH MAGICAL OILS A-Z;** Maria Solomon - $8.95
- ☐ **LOVE CHARMS & SPELLS;** Jade $6.95
- ☐ **PROTECTION CHARMS & SPELLS;** Jade - $6.95
- ☐ **MONEY MAGIC;** Jade - $6.95
- ☐ **SANTERIA; AFRICAN MAGIC IN LATIN AMERICA;** Wippler $14.95
- ☐ **RITUALS AND SPELLS OF SANTERIA;** Wippler $9.95
- ☐ **SANTERIA EXPERIENCE;** Wippler $12.95
- ☐ **MAGICAL HERBAL BATHS OF SANTERIA;** Carlos Montenegro $7.95
- ☐ **POWERS OF THE ORISHAS;** Wippler $9.95
- ☐ **THE BOOK ON PALO;** Raul Canizares $21.95
- ☐ **BRAZILIAN PALO PRIMER:** Robert Laremy $6.95
- ☐ **AGANJU; The Orisha of Volcanoes & Wilderness;** Canizares $5.95
- ☐ **ESHU ELLEGGUA; Santeria and the Orisha of the Crossroad;** Canizares $5.95
- ☐ **SHANGO; Santeria and the Orisha of Thunder;** Canizares $5.95
- ☐ **BABALU AYE; Santeria and the Lord of Pestilence;** Canizares $5.95
- ☐ **OSHUN: Santeria and the Orisha of Love;** Canizares $5.95
- ☐ **OGUN: Santeria and the Warrior Orisha of Iron;** Canizares $5.95
- ☐ **OYA: Santeria and the Orisha of Storms;** Canizares $5.95
- ☐ **YEMAYA: Santeria and the Orisha of the Seven Seas;** Canizares $5.95
- ☐ **ORUNLA: Santeria and the Orisha of Divination;** Canizares $5.95
- ☐ **OSANYIN: Santeria and the Orisha of Lord of Plants;** Canizares $5.95
- ☐ **OBATALA: Santeria and the White Robed King of the Orisha;** Canizares $5.95

NAME _____   TELEPHONE _____

ADDRESS _____

CITY _____   STATE _____   ZIP _____

AMERICAN EXPRESS VISA DISCOVER MasterCard.   **TOLL FREE (888) 622-8581 -OR- (631) 420-4053**

TO ORDER BY MAIL: CHECK THE BOXES NEXT TO YOUR SELECTIONS. ADD THE TOTAL. SHIPPING COSTS ARE $3.50 FOR
THE FIRST BOOK PLUS 75 CENTS FOR EACH ADDITIONAL BOOK. NEW YORK STATE RESIDENTS PLEASE ADD 8.25%
SALES TAX. ALL ORDERS SHIP IN 14 DAYS. SORRY, NO C.O.D.'S. SEND ORDERS TO THE ADDRESS BELOW.

ORIGINAL PUBLICATIONS • P.O. BOX 236, OLD BETHPAGE, NY 11804-0236